Britain
Guided Weapons

CHRIS GIBSON

KEY
Books

Front cover image: A Eurofighter Typhoon carrying the type's principal guided weapons. These include two Raytheon Paveway IV LGBs, six single-mode MBDA Brimstone air-to-surface missiles, four MBDA Meteor beyond visual range air-to-air missiles, two MBDA ASRAAM short range air-to-air missiles and a pair of drop tanks. (MoD/Open Government Licence)

Back cover image: Avro Vulcan B2s, such as XL427 from 617 Squadron, carried the British nuclear deterrent in the form of the Avro Blue Steel. Overflying RAF Gaydon towards the end of the missile's service in September 1969, XL427 carries a Blue Steel practice/training round. (Terry Panopalis Collection)

Title page image: One of the finest British guided weapons is Rapier, with the ultimate model of Rapier being Jernas or Field Standard C. (Blue Envoy Collection)

Contents page image: Scramble! A 5 Sqn Lightning F6 lifts off from Binbrook. Carrying a pair of de Havilland Propellors Red Top air-to-air missiles, the Lightning F6 was the last wholly British fighter carrying the last wholly British AAM. (Blue Envoy Collection)

Acknowledgements

Producing a book such as *Britain's Guided Weapons* requires teamwork, but certain individuals deserve a special mention. While few enthusiasts go out of their way to photograph guided weapons, the photographers working for the aerospace companies and the armed services do capture these important subjects and deserve a mention for their work. On the aircraft front, photographs from the collections of Phil Butler, Vic Flintham and Terry Panopalis bring the text to life. Many thanks to Jessica Brown for editing my text and, as ever, the production team at Key Publishing who provided excellent support and advice throughout.

Published by Key Books
An imprint of Key Publishing Ltd
PO Box 100
Stamford
Lincs PE19 1XQ

www.keypublishing.com

The rights of Chris Gibson to be identified as the author of this book has been asserted in accordance with the Copyright, Designs and Patents Act 1988 Sections 77 and 78.

Copyright © Chris Gibson, 2022

ISBN 978 1 80282 323 3

Typeset by SJmagic DESIGN SERVICES, India.

Contents

Introduction

Guided weapons in the United Kingdom date back to 1885, when the Brennan wire-guided torpedo and its launcher were installed at Cliffe Fort on the Hoo Peninsula in Kent. The Brennan worked, unfortunately sinking a British merchantman rather than an enemy warship. The conventional interpretation of the term 'guided weapon' is a vehicle that moves under the control of a guidance system to a target. Granted, an uninhabited air system (UAS) can do the same, but they are generally intended to return to base after their tasks, whereas guided weapons are on a one-way mission. For the purposes of this work, guided weapons that fly through the air – be they air, land, sea or subsea launched – and have been developed for service in the British armed forces will be examined. In relating this history, some coverage of equipment that was developed but not deployed is required, to provide a background to the procurement decisions on guided weapons.

Modern warfare relies on guided weapons, and they have come a long way in the century since the first Low Aerial Target (AT) flew off its ramp at Northolt in 1917. In the UK, they range from the Trident D5 strategic nuclear deterrent with multiple independently-targetable re-entry vehicles (MIRVs) that allow one submarine to deliver 64 warheads, each with a yield of up to 100kt and capable of laying waste to cities, to Martlets for destroying small inflatable boats.

The Royal Navy's first guided weapon, Sea Slug's four boosters light up the sky as it climbs away from HMS *Girdle Ness*. (Blue Envoy Collection)

Chapter 1

Origins – The Zeppelin Terror and Operation *Steinbock*

'The machine rose from the track easily, well within its length and when the tail setting has been properly adjusted, the aeroplane should be quite successful.'
Report BA.122 – Trial of 1st Aerial Target at Northolt on 6 July 1917

In January 1915, Imperial German Navy Zeppelins began a series of raids on targets in eastern England and, later, London. Intercepting these large airships proved difficult for many reasons, not least the slow rate of climb of the British fighter aircraft; and if the aircraft could reach the airships, ball and even incendiary ammunition were ineffective against the Zeppelins. The problem with the ammunition was that the .303-calibre holes did not introduce sufficient air, ie oxygen, into the airship's gas bags to allow combustion of the hydrogen; it merely produced a slow leak that the Zeppelin could cope with. There was a need to introduce more air, which required a bigger hole.

The solution to both was fast-climbing interceptors, such as modified Sopwith Camels, and the development of the Pomeroy round. Prior to these entering service, among the schemes developed to destroy the Zeppelins were the Fiery Grapnel, Low AT and Brock Rocket. The former comprised a long wire with explosive-laden grappling irons on each end, deployed by a Royal Aircraft Factory BE.2c or BE.12. The aircraft would use a winch to lower one hook, which would trail below and behind as the BE.2c flew towards the flank of the airship. The BE.2c was to pull up sharply and fly over the Zeppelin, allowing the grappling iron to tear into the envelope and gas bags and become snagged on the structure.

Zeppeline über London. A new warfare with new technology. When the Imperial German Navy's Zeppelins first appeared in the skies over Britain, there was little that could be done other than light them up with searchlights. The best engineers and scientists in the land soon developed weapons to use against them. (Blue Envoy Collection)

The attachments for the second hook would be sheared, releasing it from the aircraft and attaching to the opposite flank of the Zeppelin. The explosive charges would then detonate, and hydrogen escaping from the large gashes in the envelope and gas bags would mix with the atmosphere and burn, causing a conflagration that would engulf the Zeppelin.

The Fiery Grapnel was not a guided weapon, but the Low AT was. Designed by Archibald Low at the Royal Flying Corps Experimental Works, the AT was a small radio-controlled monoplane that was to carry its explosive load up to a Zeppelin and crash into it. Launched from a set of rails laid out on the ground, the AT was to climb while being visually tracked by an operator, with course corrections transmitted to the AT by radio until it collided with the Zeppelin. The early trials in July 1917 resulted in three crashes, but the machine was considered to be a 'viable weapon'.

The Brock Rocket was under development by Commander Frank Brock, a director of the fireworks company C T Brock & Co. It was propelled by a solid rocket motor in the forward portion of the vehicle and could be either wire or radio controlled. The Brock Rocket's guidance system was based on the equipment used on the Low AT, and control commands were executed by moving a shroud in the vehicle's nose that deflected the efflux of the rocket motor.

Low's equipment also found its way into other machines intended as anti-Zeppelin weapons. The Ruston Proctor AT was designed by Henry Folland at the Royal Aircraft Establishment (RAE) and built by the Ruston Proctor traction engine company in Lincoln, while Sopwith's Harry Hawker produced a small biplane AT that would be reworked into 'the piloted Sparrow aircraft'.

Improvements in aircraft performance and warning networks, coupled with developments such as the Pomeroy and Brock bullets that incorporated an explosive charge, proved to be the Zeppelins' nemeses. The Zeppelins were supplemented by Gotha G.IV bombers from March 1917 and Zeppelin-Staaken Riesenflugzeuge aircraft (R-planes) from September 1917. The last raid on the UK was a four-Zeppelin raid in August 1918, with one of the Zeppelins being destroyed. Had the war continued beyond 1918, guided weapons such as the Low AT and Brock Rocket could have revolutionised Great Britain's air defences.

Since bullets did not let enough air in, a bigger hole was required. The Fiery Grapnel, seen here without its explosive charges, was to be carried aloft on a BE.2c or BE.12. The reels for the cables and the controls can be seen on the fuselage side. The pilot (to save weight, there was no observer) controlled the lowering and release of the grapnels. (TNA)

The Royal Navy, always keen to embrace new technologies, turned to remotely piloted/operated aircraft in 1921 when the RAE Aerial Target (known as the RAE 1921 AT) was test flown. Intended as a target for ships' anti-aircraft guns, the AT was also considered an 'aerial torpedo', and, once the guidance equipment and catapult launch techniques were perfected, development as a weapon was considered, but under the control of a 'shepherd' aircraft. Unfortunately, the 45hp (34kW) ABC-Gnat engine proved unreliable and was replaced by an Armstrong Siddeley Ounce with the same output, while the shepherd technique was not viable in practice.

This led to the Larynx, a larger, longer-range machine powered by a 187hp (139kW) Armstrong Siddeley Lynx (hence the name – Long-Range gun with Lynx engine), and rather than a shepherd aircraft, an autopilot was fitted. Trials were conducted using the destroyers HMS *Stronghold* and HMS *Thanet* as launch platforms and the Larynx produced mixed results. Nonetheless, eventually, as the lessons from earlier flights were applied, it looked promising.

Former Prime Minister Stanley Baldwin had, in 1932, informed the House of Commons that aviation technology had reached a point where no matter what defences were ranged against them, 'the bomber will always get through'. The Air Ministry issued Specification F.5/34 for an aircraft armed

Right: **This wooden model of the Low Aerial Target may be the first guided weapon tested in a wind tunnel. Professor Low's AT suffered the same fate as many of Britain's early guided weapons – overtaken by events. (Blue Envoy Collection)**

Below: **A Larynx ready to launch, possibly on HMS *Stronghold*. Larynx was intended for use on Royal Navy warships as an anti-ship missile or against land targets as a cruise missile. It used the control systems developed by Archibald Low for the Low AT. (Via Phil Butler)**

with eight machine guns to defend against bombers (oddly enough, they were French bombers as the German Luftwaffe had yet to be revealed). In 1935, the RAE and Air Staff were also considering a guided weapon for use against bomber formations, and since this would use the shepherd technique, it was called Ram.

The Ram was to carry a 500lb (227kg) warhead at speeds of up to 400mph (644km/h), to catch up with enemy high-speed bombers. The Ram would be guided by two aircraft: the first was called the Shepherd, which flew in trail and controlled the Ram's line and elevation, while a second aircraft, the Flanker, flew abeam of the Ram and the bombers to ensure the Ram was in the ideal position within the formation before detonating the charge. Ultimately, multi-gun fighters, such as the Hurricane and Spitfire, would prove the best defence against bombers, and their use in the Battle of Britain showed that Baldwin's statement from 1932 was not to be taken as gospel.

Wartime Missiles

The received wisdom on guided weapons development during World War Two is that the Germans held all the cards, and their guided weapons (note that the V-1 and V-2 were *not* guided) were superior to anything the Allies, particularly the British, had in development. It was widely believed the British put little effort into guided weapons, but this is not accurate. The British work was innovative and could have proved more practical as weapons than anything developed in Germany.

Two roles drove guided weapons development on both sides: the interception of bombers and the destruction of ships. The German guided weapons, such as Fritz X and Hs 293, were developed to attack Allied warships from outside the ships' defences, while the burgeoning Allied bomber offensive drove development of anti-aircraft missiles such as the Enzian, Wasserfall and Rheintochter. These and other German advanced weapons have subsequently become colloquially known as *Wunderwaffen*.

In Britain, guided weapons development was similarly driven and research, particularly into anti-aircraft weapons, waxed and waned in response to the perceived threat to the UK. The British had an advantage in possessing radar systems that were more advanced than German systems, and by using centimetric radars, they could direct weapons with greater precision. Even before the introduction of centimetric radars, radar guidance was viewed as superior to the optically tracked/radio-command guidance systems used by the German weapons.

Following on from the Ram, and in the light of the Battle of Britain and ongoing Blitz, work at the Air Defence Research and Development Establishment led, in early 1941, to L H Bedford of A C Cossor Ltd drawing up a 'pilotless interceptor'. A small, uncrewed aircraft similar to the Ram was to be used as an interceptor, but rather than being visually tracked and steered by shepherds, the interceptor and its target would each be tracked by GL (Gun Laying) Mk. III radars. Commands were to be transmitted to the interceptor by radio until the two radar returns merged. The interceptor was also fitted with a rocket motor to boost it into the target before detonating the charge.

As might be expected, a pilotless interceptor based on an aircraft needed time to climb to meet the bombers and required a pair of radars at a time when every set was invaluable. The interceptors would also need to be built using a workforce and materials that could be better utilised for piloted fighters. Bedford and his colleagues at Cossors, working with Anti-Aircraft Command, set to work on a new anti-aircraft weapon, but it would take a while to perfect, as the RAE and Cossor opted for a quicker solution – rockets.

The RAE had been testing various guidance and seeker systems for anti-aircraft rockets based on the 3in (76mm) unrotated projectile (3in UP). Propelled by a solid rocket motor, these unguided rockets carried a 4lb 4oz (1.94kg) warhead and were ripple-fired from Z-batteries sited around targets, supplementing the anti-aircraft (AA) guns. The Z-batteries were not particularly effective, but the

3in rocket spawned a variety of applications, most notably the 3in rotated projectile made famous by its use by the Hawker Typhoon. Unlike the Germans, the British had no access to liquid-fuelled rocket engines, so while German engineers could develop large weapons propelled by powerful rocket engines, the British had to use the 3in rocket motor. Whereas, at first glance, this might appear to be a disadvantage, it led to more innovative applications.

Among these were the Spaniels, guided variants of the 3in UP developed by the Projectile Development Establishment. Two lines of development were pursued for ground-to-air defence: the Photo-electric (PE) Spaniel and the Radio Direction Finding (RDF) Spaniel, while a further project, the Fighter Controlled Spaniel, was developed for air-to-air use. The PE Spaniel used a photo-electric cell installed in a pod on a wing tip to act as a seeker, homing in on the silhouette of enemy aircraft. The RDF Spaniel was a beam rider, so called because it 'flew' up the beam of a centimetric gun-laying radar set that tracked the target.

Meanwhile at the RAE, engineers led by Flt Lt B S Benson were working on Ben which, like the PE Spaniel, used photo-electric cells. However, unlike the PE Spaniel, Ben could be used at night and, like the RDF variant, was a beamrider. Prior to the development of centimetric fire control radars, metric radar systems were used to direct searchlights onto bombers, with the final adjustments made manually to track the bomber once it was illuminated. Ben used backwards-facing photo-electric cells at the tips of each of the four wings and once launched would be gathered – brought under control – and moved into the searchlight beam. The missile automatically manoeuvred to keep the light intensity balanced between the four photocells and thus kept the missile in the centre of the beam as it climbed under the power of two 3in rocket motors towards the target. Ben's searchlight beam guidance would have been replaced by a radar system like the RDF Spaniel.

By summer 1942, the Luftwaffe's bomber force was otherwise engaged in the Soviet Union, and raids on the UK diminished, as did the effort to develop anti-aircraft missiles in Britain. However, in January 1944, Operation *Steinbock* commenced, with the Luftwaffe attacking targets in southern England, adding impetus to development of British air defences.

Operation *Steinbock*, April 1944. A Ben searchlight-guided missile soars into the night sky to intercept a Junkers Ju 188. The guidance and control cues came from the photocells on the tip of each wing. (Adrian Mann)

Two teams, one led by L H Bedford at Cossors and another headed up by Lt Col H B Sedgefield and Maj W E Scott of the Royal Electrical and Mechanical Engineers (REME) had quite independently conceived a beam-riding method for guiding a rocket using radar. In mid-1942, the two teams joined forces and, with the backing of General Officer Commanding Anti-Aircraft Command, Gen Frederick Pile, developed Brakemine. Described as Pile's pet project, Brakemine addressed the limitations of Ben and the Spaniels, and thanks to its six 3in rocket motors was larger, faster, longer ranged and had more development potential. Trials commenced in September 1944 and its innovations included twist and steer controls and the use of radio telemetry to monitor trials.

At the RAE, Flt Lt Benson's attention had turned to an air-to-air weapon, which became known as Artemis. Also based on the 3in rocket projectile, Artemis used the rocket's inherent rolling behaviour to produce a rotating seeker that scanned a conical volume of airspace ahead of the rocket. Artemis was a semi-active radar homing (SARH) missile that homed in on the reflected radar return from a target illuminated by the launch aircraft's radar, while another project, Little Ben, was larger but used beam-riding guidance.

Meanwhile, in the Pacific theatre, the US Navy (USN) and British Pacific Fleet were being battered by the kamikaze, whose determined attacks were proving difficult to defend against through conventional means. Standing patrols of interceptors could destroy the inbound aircraft but some would always get through. Anti-aircraft guns on ships threw up a wall of shrapnel but, in the case of the kamikaze, once in a terminal dive, even if the aircraft was destroyed, the bomb could continue its trajectory. To destroy the aircraft and its bomb, a projectile with a larger warhead than a 40mm Bofors or the 4.5in (102mm) and 5in (127mm) AA guns used by the ships was needed.

A committee was established to examine guided anti-aircraft projectiles and became known as the GAP Committee, which increased its scope and began to look into guided weapons for the British armed services. The Admiralty was already looking to guided weapons to provide defence for its ships and had commenced a project called Sea Slug in 1943 to counter Luftwaffe aircraft that launched anti-ship missiles such as the Fritz X and Hs 293. This looked like it would take too long to develop (most prescient on the Admiralty's part) so the Admiralty took over a British Army

General Pile's pet project, the Cossor/ REME/AA Command Brakemine, on its launcher, a modified 3.7in AA gun mount. Brakemine pioneered techniques that would be used on post-war SAMs and their development. (REME Museum)

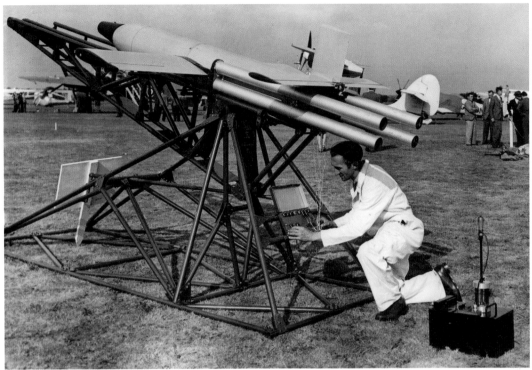

Fairey's Stooge in launch configuration. The Stooge control system may have its origins in an earlier Admiralty project for a radio-controlled glider for laying smoke screens. The long tubes at the rear are 3in (7.6cm) boost rocket motors, while the dark 'plant pot' on the nose is a weight to balance the boosters. These all fall away when the boost motors burn out. (Blue Envoy Collection)

project called Stooge: a small rocket-powered monoplane designed by Fairey. The optically tracked, command-guided Stooge was powered by four Mayfly 5in (127mm) rocket motors in the tail and boosted off its launch stand by four 3in (76mm) rocket motors.

Meanwhile, and possibly the reason the army handed Stooge to the navy, Brakemine was showing promise. It looked the part and was fitted with a beam-riding guidance system driving twist/steer controls and provided an all-weather capability with a long range that was unavailable with optical

Fairey's Stooge in flight configuration. The missile would be powered by four 5in (12.7cm) Swallow sustainer rocket motors and guided by an operator on the ship. Flares in the wingtips helped the operator to track the weapon. (Blue Envoy Collection)

guidance/manual control. Brakemine was launched from a modified 3.7in (94mm) AA gun mounting with guidance from a gun-laying radar, such as Radar, Anti-Aircraft, No 3 or the American SCR-584.

With the end of hostilities, the teams working on guided weapons for the services were broken up and, on returning to their various aircraft companies, their research ticking over, produced a plethora of design studies and proposals. The GAP Committee continued its work, examining propulsion and guidance systems, and, aside from the Admiralty's Sea Slug, there were no official requirements for guided weapons. In 1947, the disparate projects came under the aegis of the Ministry of Supply (MOS) and the RAE.

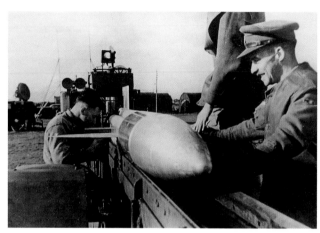

Left: REME officers and Cossor engineers make the final checks on a Brakemine surface-to-air guided weapon prior to a test launch. Three of the sextet of 3in rocket motors can be seen at the rear of the missile. The vehicle's size is most apparent, especially when compared with contemporary German weapons such as Wasserfall. (REME Museum)

Below: At sea, the Royal Navy's first-generation SAM was Sea Slug. The size of the system is evident from the officer in White No 1 Dress standing beside the launcher of HMS *London* on a visit to Singapore. The launcher is aligned with the doors leading to the large and complex handling system inside the hull. (Blue Envoy Collection)

Chapter 2

The Forty-Niners and the Early Steps

'... no further attempts at a cannon solution for medium or heavy anti-aircraft defence'.

Ministry of Supply policy statement, 1958

It was time to put the band back together. The Soviets had, in August 1949, detonated their first atomic bomb, Joe 1, and had a means of delivery in the form of the Tupolev Tu-4 *Bull*, a reverse-engineered Boeing B-29 Superfortress. The British had embarked on their own nuclear weapon and delivery systems programmes in August 1945 and were faced with the prospect of one aircraft, possibly even a supersonic jet, laying waste to a city. British air defences needed an interception capability. Anti-aircraft artillery, even the 5in (127mm) Green Mace gun with a rate of fire of 96 rounds per minute, could not stop a bomber before it released its weapon – that required surface-to-air guided weapons (SAGWs) and interceptors armed with air-to-air guided weapons (AAGWs).

As ever, interservice rivalry came to the fore, which would ultimately see different requirements discussed and dismissed until, in the light of events in 1949 (the Soviet bomb test and establishment of NATO), the situation became focused. Clement Attlee's government had applied a 'Super Priority' label to the atom bomb project and its delivery systems and, faced with a need to defend these, applied the same priority to a SAGW.

The overall plan was to develop the UK's air defences in three stages: Stage 1 with a range of 20 miles (32km), essentially protecting the bomber bases; Stage 2, with a range of 200 miles (320km), was to protect the main population centres; while Stage 3, added later, was somewhat vague and would be too complex to define in 1949.

Guided weapons were the future, but viewed with some suspicion by many, not just the aircrew who saw them as a threat to their status and 'stick time'. (De Havilland Gazette via BAE Systems)

'Well, I'm working on a rocket now which goes up to 30,000ft, shoots down the enemy, comes back to base, reports to the debriefing room, and then shoots a line about itself in the mess.'

The RAF was tasked with the air defence of the UK and opted to let the contract for Stage 1 to Bristol Aircraft (airframe and propulsion) and Ferranti (guidance). The Bristol team became known as 'The Forty-Niners' and proceeded to develop a ramjet-powered missile called Red Duster, later known as Bloodhound. The General Staff wanted a missile to defend the army in the field from air attack and, despite an initial order for Red Duster, turned to English Electric (airframe and guidance) and Napier (propulsion) to develop Red Shoes, which became Thunderbird.

The Red Duster programme that produced Bloodhound involved a huge number of experimental test vehicles, known as XTVs. This XTV.4 has just been launched and the ramjets are about to light up. (Blue Envoy Collection)

Bristol brothers in arms. The loadmaster of Bristol Belvedere HC1 XG451 monitors a Bloodhound I SAM being lifted for a publicity shot. Bloodhound I entered RAF service in 1958 to defend the V-bomber bases in eastern England. Like most of the first generation of British guided weapons, they provided the service with experience rather than a true capability. (Blue Envoy Collection)

As for air-to-air weapons, requirement OR.1056 was issued for an active-homing weapon to arm RAF interceptors. Gloster drew up a complex active-homing weapon called Red Hawk – essentially a small aircraft, which was far removed from the compact Artemis and Little Ben designs of wartime. This was assessed by the RAE and deemed too complicated, so in 1949, Red Hawk was 'diluted' to become Pink Hawk and, on transfer to Fairey Aviation, became a beam-riding weapon called Blue Sky, which entered limited service on the Supermarine Swift F7 as the Fairey Fireflash.

Red Hawk continued for a short time before being split into the active-seeking Red Dean and the infrared (IR) homing Blue Jay, with requirements OR.1105 and OR.1117 issued to cover these. Red Dean was being developed by Folland, but the RAE and MOS thought their chief engineer, W E W 'Teddy' Petter, was not applying sufficient vigour to the work, so Red Dean was transferred to Vickers. A massive weapon, Red Dean was to be carried by the Gloster Thin-Wing Javelin, but both were overtaken (such was the slow pace of British missile development) by the weapon system based around the F.155 specification. The Fairey Delta III interceptor to F.155 was to be armed with the Vickers Red

Right: **A Blue Sky AAM during trials on a Gloster Meteor NF11. The two Stork boost motors are attached top and bottom, with the nozzles slightly canted to impart stabilising spin on the unpowered dart. (Blue Envoy Collection)**

Below: **A Fairey Firefly U8 on display with a Blue Sky AAM at an airshow in the early 1950s. Fairey used drone conversions of their Firefly fighter as targets during Blue Sky trials, and the Firefly was a regular target for British anti-aircraft missiles. The wing pods housed cameras. (Blue Envoy Collection)**

Hebe missile that was even bigger than Red Dean. The Delta III itself was not much smaller than an Avro Vulcan, while Red Hebe is probably the largest AAM ever proposed at 22ft 10in (6.96m) long with its aerodynamic fairings. Red Hebe was beaten only by the Soviet R-40 (NATO reporting name: AA-6 *Acrid*) that entered service on the MiG-25 *Foxbat*, the Soviet equivalent of the F.155 interceptor.

The infrared-guided Blue Jay developed by de Havilland Propellers to meet OR.1117 was the only one of these early British AAMs to enter operational service, becoming the Firestreak that armed the English Electric Lightning, Gloster Javelin and de Havilland Sea Vixen.

All of these early British AAMs shared one feature: size. Compared with their American contemporaries, British AAMs were around twice the weight of the American equivalents – Sparrow and Sidewinder. One RAF officer familiar with the American weapons, Sqn Ldr Poole, described the British devices as being from the 'piston age'. Poole was correct, certainly from an industrial point of view, but as a weapon to meet the RAF's needs, Firestreak was what they required: a weapon with a large warhead that could destroy a Soviet subsonic bomber. Firestreak was the sharp end of a weapons system that, when combined with ground-controlled interception systems, put the interceptor behind a Soviet

Not all guided weapon development involves test vehicles and aircraft. The infrared seeker for Blue Jay was tested against a series of gas-fired heaters mounted on scaffolding. Shorts fired the Green Light test vehicle at bales of straw because they had no test range. (Blue Envoy Collection)

De Havilland's Blue Jay was flight tested on the same company's Venom NF2 WL813 and, later, WL820. Air-firing trials began in April 1953, with the first fully guided firing in September 1955. De Havilland's AAMs would be in service for another 30 years. (Blue Envoy Collection)

between the missile pairs. The optical controller unit is separated from the fire unit and is fitted with optical and TV trackers, the latter providing the guidance cues to the missile.

Rapier entered service with the RAF Regiment in 1974, replacing the Shorts Tigercat, which the Regiment had fielded since 1968, essentially as a stopgap after Mauler was cancelled, pending delivery of Rapier. It came as no surprise that a weapons system designed only for clear weather operation was less than ideal in northern Europe. This was addressed in 1970 by the development of the DN.181 Blindfire radar, oddly enough at the behest of the Imperial Iranian Army, who received Blindfire in 1973 – six years before British users. Once the Blindfire radar was added to Rapier, it was designated Field Standard A (FSA).

Right: Pending delivery of Rapier, the Shorts Tigercat was deployed for local air defence of airfields. A land-based version of Sea Cat, the fire unit comprised a three-round launcher and a fire director. (Blue Envoy Collection)

Below: Introduced to the British Army in 1979, the DN.181 Blindfire radar gave Rapier an all-weather capability by tracking both missile and target. The addition of Blindfire produced Rapier Field Standard A (FSA). (Blue Envoy Collection)

Another Rapier variant, again developed at the request of Iran, was the Tracked Rapier, which originally mounted the fire unit on a modified M548 cargo carrier, with the trackers in an enlarged cab. This was soon changed to a new bespoke armoured fire unit with four missiles in armoured bins on each side of the fire unit turret. The new carrier was called RCM.748, while the Blindfire radar was carried on a separate RCM.748. These entered British Army service in 1983, but only because the Iranian order was cancelled after the Iranian Revolution of 1979. Rapier first saw action in Iranian service, destroying an Iraqi Air Force Ilyushin Il-76 *Candid* in 1974, possibly operated by British contractors. The system also engaged and destroyed Iraqi aircraft during the Iran–Iraq War of 1980–88.

Rapier saw extensive use in the 1982 Falklands Conflict, though with initial exaggeration of its success – 14 Argentine aircraft claimed destroyed. Ultimately, the variety and number of SAMs fired made assigning claims to specific missiles very difficult. The official line is that one aircraft was definitely shot down by Rapier, with two probable and two possible kills. Rapier was not unique in this confusion; there were lots of SAMs in the air over the Falkland Islands in May 1982.

Lessons from the Falklands were incorporated into later developments, including Field Standard B (FSB) with system upgrades and Laserfire, which used a laser radar (LIDAR) rather than a radar to track the target and missile and a millimetre wave (MMW) radar for warning. These changes made the

Rapier was portable, towed by a 1-tonne FC Land Rover or airlifted by helicopter. Both are shown here, as a Chinook HC1 ZA672 lifts a 1-tonne Land Rover and Rapier fire unit into position. (Blue Envoy Collection)

system small enough to be palletised and carried on a truck, *a la* PT.428. A further variant, known as Darkfire, incorporated a thermal imager that enabled Rapier to operate at night.

The missile itself was also upgraded, with new rocket motors and warheads, including a proximity fuse to deal with small targets such as UAS. A new warhead was developed, including the Mk. 2B that has a shaped charge for use against lightly armoured vehicles such as APCs, and enemy mobile anti-aircraft systems such as self-propelled anti-aircraft guns (SPAAGs).

Rapier 2000, also known as Jernas (Arabic for 'a falcon in its prime'), for the export market or Rapier Field Standard C (FSC) in the British Army, was virtually a different system with a new optical tracker mounted on top of the fire unit and an Alenia Marconi Dagger 3D pulse doppler radar on a separate trailer. The new fire unit and separate radar allowed the number of deployed missiles to be increased from four to eight. Rapier remained in service until 2021, when it was replaced by the MBDA Sky Sabre, with the Land Ceptor variant of the Common Anti-air Modular Missile (CAMM) as the missile.

Right: **An RAF Phantom cleans up as it takes off from an airfield under the protection of Rapier. The crew are in full NBC kit for an exercise. The salient features of the early Rapier can be seen here: fire unit with command antenna, optical tracker on a tripod and the SEZ box. The SEZ (Selector Engagement Zone) box has a circular array of 32 lamps, which light up to indicate the direction of a target. (Blue Envoy Collection)**

Below: **A Fairchild A-10A Thunderbolt II of the USAF Reserve Command taxies past a Rapier FSC unit on a UK airfield. The differences between the original fire unit and that of Rapier FSC are apparent here, including the eight-round launcher and new tracker. Rapiers, with British crews, provided air defence for American airfields during the Cold War. (Blue Envoy Collection)**

Sky Sabre replaces Rapier with the British Army's air defence unit. A Sky Sabre unit comprises a Giraffe radar, control vehicle and launch vehicle. Each launcher carries eight launch cells for Land Ceptor missiles. (MOD/Open Government Licence)

Dagger to ATASK – MANPADS

By the mid-1960s, thanks to great strides in miniaturisation and the development of transistorised systems, an unprecedented reduction in the size of guided weapons was achieved. This was particularly true with anti-aircraft and anti-tank missiles, to such an extent that one or two soldiers could carry and operate weapons against a foe that was previously untouchable.

In 1964, Shorts presented the MOD with a proposal for what is now called a 'man-portable air defence system' (MANPADS), based on a test vehicle they called Blowpipe. Unlike the contemporary

US and Soviet MANPADS, Redeye and Strela that used infrared guidance, the Blowpipe test vehicle used visual command guidance similar to Sea Cat. Shorts claimed this could be used against approaching or crossing targets, whereas infrared missiles required the aircraft to pass, revealing its hot jet pipe. Shorts also pointed out that it could be used against low-infrared signature aircraft such as helicopters.

The army and navy liked Blowpipe but, sceptical of the army's aircraft recognition skills, the RAF demanded

The General Staff in the late 1960s compared Shorts' MANPADS with SPAAGS such as the Falcon. The guided weapon won as it was deemed more flexible, more effective, required fewer resources and was considerably cheaper. Blowpipe née... Blowpipe (via Dagger and RF.268) gave the British Army a small unit air defence capability. Visual guidance allowed its use against approaching aircraft and those with low infrared signatures. It was also very handy against vehicles! (Blue Envoy Collection)

Typical of the first generation of SAMs, the Armstrong Whitworth/GEC Sea Slug taught the Royal Navy many lessons in operating guided weapons and along the way acquired new propulsion systems, changing to a solid rocket motor sustainer from a liquid-fuelled engine. HMS *Girdle Ness*, a repair ship, was converted to act as the trials ship for Sea Slug and confirmed that the missile was cumbersome – each round had to be prepared, checked, boosters added and moved onto the launcher before firing. The GWS-1 Sea Slug was fitted to the eight County-class destroyers that were essentially built around the system, making them almost as large as a cruiser. A single two-round launcher was mounted towards the stern of the ship, and when slewed aft, lined up with blast-proof doors that allowed missiles to be passed from the magazine to the launcher. Missile launches were spectacular affairs that generally involved slewing the launcher athwartships to avoid blast damage to the ship. The last two ships of the class in the Royal Navy, *Antrim* and *Glamorgan*, served in the Falklands Conflict of 1982, where Sea Slug operated against aircraft and land targets, including a radar.

Any warship would be dominated by the assembly line of the Sea Slug system and, despite having entered development in 1943, it was only declared operational in 1961, by which time all technologies related to guided weapons had moved on.

While Sea Slug was intended to defend the fleet against high-altitude bombers with free-fall nuclear weapons, as the developments in strike aircraft progressed in the 1950s, the new threat to the fleet became smaller aircraft operating at low-level, epitomised by the Blackburn Buccaneer. The Admiralty had already considered this, but in the mid-1940s, the threat was the kamikaze or torpedo attacks by aircraft. In 1945, the defences against 'close in' threats comprised the quad QF 2-pdr 'Pom-Pom' and the 40mm Bofors in multi-barrel mounts. The Admiralty's initial thinking was to equip all the ships in a convoy with missiles called Popsy and use a control ship equipped with a radar and guidance system to co-ordinate the defence, but this was deemed impractical.

Seagulls gather around HMS *Girdle Ness* as it sets out for sea trials. For much of Sea Slug's tortuous testing and trials, HMS *Girdle Ness*, a highly modified repair ship, was used for launching Sea Slugs against drone variants of Fireflies, Meteors and Canberras. (Blue Envoy Collection)

Powered by a Sealyham motor, a Shorts Sea Cat leaves the quad launcher on a Royal Navy destroyer. The elongated radome on the mount covers the command control antenna. Later variants incorporated improved fire control and guidance systems. (Blue Envoy Collection)

To replace Popsy, a new missile called Orange Nell was proposed, but this used a launch system almost as complicated as Sea Slug. This was deemed far too complex for what was effectively a weapon that could replace the Bofors mounts on ships, so the focus turned to a missile derived from work on an optically tracked infrared-guided anti-tank missile called Orange William and its successor, the Australian wire-guided Malkara (see Chapter 8). Too big and deemed unusable in the smoke and general fog of war on a battlefield, Shorts took the basic Malkara configuration and commenced development of Green Light, which led to the GWS.20 Sea Cat, an optically tracked, radio-command, short-range anti-aircraft missile.

Sea Cat's quad launcher was more or less a straight replacement for the STAAG (Stabilised Tachometric Anti-Aircraft Gun) on warships; it was much lighter and required less maintenance than the quad gun mount. With a range of up to 3 miles (5km), Sea Cat could tackle subsonic strike aircraft and the early Soviet anti-ship missiles.

The GWS.20 entered service in 1962 on HMS *Corunna*, a Battle-class destroyer, and as the 1960s progressed, versions such as the GWS.21 and GWS.22 with improved tracking using radar and closed-circuit television appeared. The final variant, GWS.24 with automatic gathering onto the target, entered service on the Type 21 Amazon-class in 1974. Sea Cat led to the land-based Tigercat used by the RAF Regiment for airfield defence while the Rapier was being developed.

The Next Generation: Darts and Wolves

If Sea Slug's size and mode of operation had taught the Admiralty one lesson, it was that any future guided weapons should be handled like the ammunition of the ship's big guns. Rather than moving along the equivalent of an aircraft production line, new missiles should be self-contained and stored in magazines, with mechanised loading onto compact trainable launchers – just like the gun turrets of the battleships that aircraft had sent to the bottom of the oceans or the scrapyard – with each launcher combining the weapons platform and ammunition storage.

The Admiralty had ideas about how a more compact air defence system should be achieved, and Bristol Aircraft drew up the New Integrated Guided-weapon System, known as NIGS. Bristol proposed a delta-winged missile with two ramjets to provide the necessary 50 miles (80km) range, but NIGS was deemed too big by the Admiralty. This led to the Small Ships Guided-Weapon System (SIGS), a small ramjet-powered missile with a gothic arch delta wing.

The SIGS configuration did not lend itself to the ammunition handling systems envisioned by the Admiralty, but the Bristol Odin Ramjet and guidance systems were included in a new airframe design for a missile system to be developed by Armstrong Whitworth. The Ministry of Aviation assigned the designation CF.299 to the project, but it is better known as Sea Dart.

Compared with Sea Slug, the Sea Dart system was very compact. Missiles were stored vertically in a 22-round (38 rounds in HMS *Bristol*) magazine and, when required, hoisted up to a twin-rail launcher that, once loaded, could be trained in azimuth and elevation under direction of the fire control system to point the missile towards the target. A Type 965 radar (replaced by the Type 1022) surveillance radar detected the target which was then illuminated by a Type 909 radar.

Once the target had been acquired, Sea Dart was boosted off the launcher by a Chow solid rocket motor that propelled the missile to the supersonic speed required to light the ramjet sustainer engine. The Bristol Siddeley Odin ramjet powered the missile to Mach 3.5, and by using a kerosene-fuelled ramjet, the Sea Dart could maintain its speed and manoeuvrability until impacting the target.

The GWS-30 Sea Dart entered service on HMS *Bristol* in 1973 and served with distinction in the Falklands Conflict of 1982, shooting down seven Argentine aircraft and an Exocet anti-ship missile. During the operations to liberate Kuwait in 1991, Sea Dart launched by the Type 42 destroyer HMS *Gloucester* destroyed a HY-2 *Silkworm* missile fired at USS *Missouri*, which was providing fire support for land operations.

The Chow booster propels a Sea Dart off the launch rail during trials at Woomera. To be handled like naval rifle ammunition, the GWS-30 Sea Dart was a fraction of the size and weight of Sea Slug. (Blue Envoy Collection)

Not quite as smoky as a Sea Slug launch, the Chow boost motor on Hawker Siddeley's Sea Dart envelops its launcher in smoke. HMS *Edinburgh* made the last Sea Dart launch. The only one of Britain's 'heavy' SAMs to destroy enemy aircraft in combat, Sea Dart was a huge improvement on Sea Slug. (MOD/Open Government Licence)

While Sea Dart's anti-missile capability was very much a bonus, the Admiralty had seen the need to counter the threat posed by low-flying aircraft and sea-skimming anti-ship missiles. Confessor was the name given to a series of studies to replace Sea Cat that led to the phenomenal BAC Sea Wolf point-defence system. By the convention that a confessor must be a sinner, a contemporary development programme called Sinner was initiated to examine a vertical launch version of the missile.

Confessor was selected for development, possibly because it was easier and cheaper than Sinner, and entered service as GWS-25 Sea Wolf on the Type 22 Broadsword-class in 1979. Each frigate carried a pair of six-box trainable launchers, meaning the ship had 12 Sea Wolves available. However, prior to launch the launchers had to be rotated towards the threat. Sea Wolf is most famous for the quip during

To replace Sea Cat and give an enhanced capability against small close-in threats, such as sea-skimming anti-ship missiles, BAC developed Sea Wolf. Six Sea Wolf missiles were installed on a trainable launcher with three box launchers each side. (MOD/Open Government Licence)

particularly suited to the close support role, so as soon as the SEPECAT Jaguar appeared, the Phantoms moved to what they did best – air defence.

The FAA had fitted its Supermarine Scimitars with the AIM-9B Sidewinder after trials in the late 1950s, but when the Phantom FG1s arrived in 1968, they came equipped with the AIM-9G Sidewinder and AIM-7C Sparrow, as used by the US Navy.

De Havilland Sea Vixen FAW2 XN684 carries a heavy load of four Red Top air-to-air missiles and two drop tanks. The Sea Vixen FAW2 was a development of the FAW1 that carried more fuel, additional ECM equipment and avionics compatible with the Red Top and Bullpup missiles. (Blue Envoy Collection)

Right: When the F-4M Phantom FGR2 arrived in service, it was pitched into the air-to-ground tactical support role for which it was less than ideal. While the Phantom could carry a heavy warload, it could not carry it very far. The Phantoms soon transferred to air defence. (Blue Envoy Collection)

Below: The FAA was the first British armed service to adopt the AIM-9 Sidewinder for its Supermarine Scimitars. In addition to a Sidewinder, Scimitar F1 XD239 carries a Red Beard target marker on the inboard port pylon and a Flight Refuelling Ltd Mk.20 refuelling pod under the starboard wing. Possibly not an operational weapons fit. (Terry Panopalis Collection via Tony Buttler)

By the 1980s, Sidewinders, particularly the AIM-9L variant, proliferated across Britain's air forces. Types such as the Buccaneer and Jaguar were fairly obvious platforms given their role of flying into high-threat environments in eastern Europe, but the Hawker Siddeley Nimrod MR2 sporting four Sidewinders was a bit of a surprise. Another type that adopted the Sidewinder was the Hawker Siddeley Hawk T1A, with the Tactical Weapons Units' trainers working in concert with Tornado F3s in the air defence role.

The crew of 43 Sqn Phantom FG1 XV574 watch a Soviet Naval Aviation Tu-95 *Bear-D*. The cancellation of HMS *Eagle*'s refit allowed the RAF to acquire air defence Phantom FG1s diverted from the FAA. The Phantoms and their Sparrow and Sidewinder missiles much improved the RAF's air defence capability in the eastern North Atlantic. (Blue Envoy Collection)

Left: One rather unexpected addition to the Nimrod's weapon suite was the AIM-9L Sidewinder, which was described by its crews as the world's biggest fighter. Nimrod MR2 XV254, complete with inflight refuelling probe, shows off its Sidewinders over the Moray Firth. (Blue Envoy Collection)

Below: Unthinkable before 1989, an air defence configured Hawk T1A in formation with a pair of Czech Air Force Aero L39 Albatrosses and a MiG-23 *Flogger-G*. From 1983 until 1986, Hawk T1As filled a secondary short-range interceptor role with its 30mm ADEN cannon and a pair of AIM-9L Sidewinders. (Blue Envoy Collection)

A pair of Lightnings, armed with Firestreaks, escort a Soviet *Bison* in the UK ADIZ. The Myasisischev M4 *Bison* was one of the Soviet bombers that English Electric Lightning was intended to intercept with Firestreak. (Blue Envoy Collection)

Tornados and the New AAMs

From the mid-1970s, the British forces moved their focus to western Europe and the eastern North Atlantic. The RAF's role was to protect convoys from Soviet maritime strike aircraft such as the Tupolev Tu-95 *Bear*, Tu-16 *Badger* and Tu-22M *Backfire*. While this was the original role for the US Navy's Phantoms, which would have operated from aircraft carriers, the RAF's Phantom FGR2s, and later the FG1s, were land based. They relied on inflight refuelling by Handley Page Victors and airborne early warning by Avro Shackleton AEW2s (pending the arrival of the Nimrod AEW3).

What the Air Staff was now aiming for was a missile platform as per the 1964 Jones Report, carrying as many missiles as possible, which could patrol the Greenland–Iceland–UK (GIUK) Gap. It issued ASR.395, which eventually became the Tornado Air Defence Variant (ADV). At the same time, requirements for new AAMs were issued to replace the Sidewinder (ASR.1222 Short Range AAM) and Sparrow (ASR.1219 Medium Range AAM). Hawker Siddeley Dynamics (HSD, née de Havilland Propellers) had, in 1968, embarked on a new short-range infrared homing missile to replace Red Top.

Left: Kings of the North. Sentry AEW1 ZH106 and Panavia Tornado F3 ZF862 in formation. Skyflash was the sharp end of a new air defence system to defend the Greenland–Iceland–UK Gap and prevent Soviet maritime strike aircraft attacking NATO convoys. Missing here is an example of the Vickers VC10 tankers that were to support the Tornado F3 and Sentry AEW1 fleets. (Blue Envoy Collection)

Originally called Taildog, it was highly manoeuvrable and housed in a tube but, more importantly, it did not require an ammonia heat exchanger pack to cool the missile seeker. Taildog would, via a variety of abortive collaboration deals, become the MBDA ASRAAM.

Left: Red Top was a radically modified Blue Jay with improved seeker, fuze and motor. Red Top's Violet Banner seeker provided a 'limited' all-aspect capability against supersonic bombers. A cleaner design than Firestreak, Red Top carriage required the Lightning to have increased fin area, as seen on the F3 and F6 variants. (Blue Envoy Collection)

Below: De Havilland followed Red Top with Taildog, which evolved into ASRAAM via SRAAM, an agile dogfight missile with an infrared seeker. The crew of a Sea Vixen strike a pose with a pair of SRAAMs. (Blue Envoy Collection)

The ordnance array with this Lightning F53 shows Firestreak on the right and Red Top on the left. Both Firestreak and its successor, Red Top, were carried on pylons connected to a weapon pack – essentially a removable pallet that carried ancillaries for the missiles. For Firestreak, this included an ammonia cooling system. The item in front of the Lightning is a photo-reconnaissance pallet that could replace the weapons pack. It was not adopted by the RAF. (Blue Envoy Collection)

De Havilland's Firestreak and Red Top infrared homing missiles required a large cooling pack on the aircraft to cool the seekers enough to acquire a lock on the hot metal of the target. Their seekers also needed to be slaved to the aircraft radar to allow the infrared seeker to be cued up on the target. De Havilland's missiles were very much dedicated anti-bomber weapons; the AIM-9 Sidewinder on the other hand was for use against fighters, was very much self-contained and could be carried by most aircraft with little modification.

In May 1973, the Air Staff issued ASR.1222, calling for a small, agile AAM to replace the AIM-9D Sidewinder in British service. HSD embarked on the development of a dogfight missile that was, like Sidewinder, essentially self-contained and very agile. Building on the earlier work for Taildog, HSD developed SRAAM (Short Range AAM) 100 as a highly manoeuvrable tube-launched missile; it was so manoeuvrable that one trials round almost collided with the Hawker Hunter launch aircraft!

Oddly enough for an aircraft in RAF and FAA service from the 1950s, until the 1990s, the Hawker Hunter never carried operational guided weapons, even when used as a trainer for aircraft, unlike as the Sea Harrier, which carried Sidewinders. Overseas users of the Hunter did fit guided weapons, particularly the Republic of Singapore Air Force, whose Hunter FGA74s could carry up to four AIM-9 Sidewinders and, famously, the Swiss Air Force, whose Mk.58A could carry Sidewinders and the AGM-65 Maverick.

Above: As before, Hawker Hunters were used for guided weapons development. Hunter F6 XG210 was used for development flying and launch trials with the twin SRAAM launcher. (Blue Envoy Collection)

Left: Hunter FGA9s of 208 Sqn from RAF Eastleigh in Kenya perform an immaculate formation loop over the Serengeti. Despite its long service life with UK armed forces, the Hawker Hunter was never operational with guided weapons. Even the later variants, such as the F6/FGA9, were only equipped with unguided weapons and guns. (Blue Envoy Collection)

Below: Unlike the RAF and FAA, other air forces armed the Hunter with guided weapons. These included the Republic of Singapore AF and Swedish AF, which opted for Sidewinders, while the Swiss Air Force equipped it with Sidewinders and the AGM-65 Maverick. On display in the RSAF Museum at Paya Lebar, Singapore, Hawker Hunter FGA74S 527 is fitted with four dummy AIM-9 Sidewinders, drop tanks and Mk. 82 bombs. This aircraft was formerly XF458 in RAF service. (Author)

SRAAM lost out to the latest model Sidewinder, to be licence built in the UK. However, in 1979, the Air Staff subsequently issued ASR.1234 for an advanced missile called ASRAAM, this time teaming up with West Germany to develop it. This arrangement was part of a deal whereby European companies developed an infrared missile, while US companies developed a radar-guided weapon. Under the memorandum of understanding signed in the mid-1980s, the UK and West Germany would accept the AIM-120 AMRAAM, and the US would adopt ASRAAM as the AIM-132. This situation did not last long. West Germany departed from the programme in 1989, whereas the US opted to further develop the tried and tested Sidewinder to produce the AIM-9X.

This left the UK and BAeD with full authority over ASRAAM. However, under competition rules, the MOD had to elicit tenders, so in 1990 it asked the missile companies to submit their proposals. Matra's MICA and a German missile from Bodensee Geratetechnik were put forward as well as ASRAAM. The German missile would evolve into IRIS-T, but it was ASRAAM that won the RAF order and started production in 1992.

ASRAAM uses an imaging infrared seeker that benefits from a lock-on-after-launch capability and a powerful Remus rocket motor that provides both high acceleration and speed. It also confers long range on ASRAAM, reportedly up to 31 miles (50km), with inertial guidance placing a dogfight missile in the beyond-visual range category. Further enhancements to ASRAAM include P3I-ASRAAM, proposed in 1995, which added thrust vector controls to enhance agility. This variant was proposed to replace the Sidewinder in US service but, as with the AIM-132, it was not taken up, mainly due to the number of Sidewinders on the US inventory. They did, however, take the seeker and use it to upgrade thousands of earlier Sidewinders.

Initial operational capability with ASRAAM was achieved in 1998, and its first use in anger by the RAF was on 14 December 2021, when a Typhoon FGR4 used an ASRAAM to destroy a drone operated by so-called Islamic State/Daesh.

Right: Punching out flares as it banks away, a Tornado F3 from 111 Sqn carries four Skyflash missiles and at least one ASRAAM on its wing pylon. By the end of its RAF service life in 2012, the Tornado F3 was equipped with AMRAAMs and ASRAAMs, with some (unofficially designated EF3) having a SEAD capability with ALARM. (MOD/Open Government Licence)

Below: In the air defence role, RAF Typhoons were armed with ASRAAMs and AMRAAMs (pending delivery of Meteor). Typhoon FGR4 ZJ924 of XI(F) Sqn takes off from RAF Coningsby during support operations for Operation *Ellamy* carrying four ASRAAMs and four AMRAAMs. (MOD/Open Government Licence)

Missiles lend themselves to different roles and, never one to waste an opportunity to use existing technology, BAeD has used ASRAAM as the basis for several guided weapons over the years. In the 1980s, the need for protection against Warsaw Pact mobile air defences spawned the BAeD Short-Range Anti-Radiation Missile (SRARM), intended to complement rather than compete with the same company's Air-Launched Anti-Radiation Missile (ALARM).

The basic ASRAAM airframe was fitted with a tandem-charge anti-tank warhead from Trigat to produce the Typhoon, proposed for the same requirement as Brimstone. Interestingly, the Typhoon retained an anti-aircraft capability, ideal for use against helicopters, although Brimstone no doubt also has this capability.

MBDA's ASRAAM-derived proposals fared better in the 21st century under a programme called Common Anti-air Modular Missile (CAMM). The first application of CAMM was Sea Ceptor, a replacement for the Sea Wolf point-defence weapons on Royal Navy Type 23 Duke-class frigates. CAMM uses a 'soft' vertical launch, and each of the vertical launch cells previously holding one VL Sea Wolf now holds a single Sea Ceptor. The missile uses an active radar seeker and can be integrated with the PAAMS fire control system for Sea Viper on Type 45 Dauntless-class destroyers. Sea Ceptor was declared operational on HM ships in May 2018 (see Chapter 4).

For the army, the imaginatively named Land Ceptor is the business end of the British Army's Sky Sabre air defence system, which is replacing the Rapier. While not as compact and mobile as Rapier, (the SAAB Giraffe 3D surveillance radar, Rafael fire control system and launch boxes are each carried on MAN HX 8x8 15-tonne trucks), Land Ceptor has more than three times the range.

Skyflash

The contract to meet the 1972 Sparrow replacement requirement, ASR.1219, was let to HSD and Marconi, whose bid was developed as the XJ.521. This was essentially a reworked Sparrow with a new Marconi seeker, new EMI fuze and a Hoopoe rocket motor. The Marconi semi-active monopulse seeker was more jam-resistant than the Sparrow, and, significantly, it could be carried on the same mountings as the Sparrow. Once in service, XJ.521 was renamed Skyflash, and it replaced the Sparrow on Phantoms from 1978. To avoid confusion in the interim period, when Sparrow and Skyflash were both in service, Skyflash could be identified by black circles painted on the fins.

One of the Tornado F2 prototypes has just launched a Skyflash during trials. The Tornado Air Defence Variant carried its four Skyflash under the fuselage. To ensure a clean launch, Frazer Nash developed a system of 'trapezes' that pushed the missiles clear of the airframe before the Hoopoe motor fired. (Via Vic Flintham)

The AS.37 was dismissed for Operation *Black Buck 4-6* against Argentine radars during the Falklands Conflict for several reasons, not just its reliability. On the starboard side of the Vulcan is a pair of AS.37 (minus fins) and a pair of Shrikes. The size difference is apparent. (Blue Envoy Collection)

Hellcat, a variant of the Sea Cat SAM, was proposed as a helicopter-launched missile for use against the missile-armed fast patrol boats such as the Egyptian Navy Komar-class that had sent the Israeli destroyer *Eilat* to the bottom in the 1967 Six-Day War.

Shorts failed to inspire the Admiralty with Hellcat, so the FAA's Westland Wasps and Wessexes, plus RAF Nimrods, were armed with the Nord AS.12. The wire-guided AS.12 was a manual command to line-of-sight (MCLOS) missile, which meant the operator had to keep the missile in sight until it hit the target. This would work satisfactorily when launched from a helicopter but less so when launched from the Nimrod which, during the 30-second flight time, would be closing in on the target and into range of the ship's air defences. It did not last long in the Nimrod's armoury but was (fairly) successfully used in the Falklands Conflict by the Wessex and Wasp, disabling an Argentine Navy submarine and taking the roof off Port Stanley police station.

With the Wasp being replaced by the Lynx, a missile to replace the AS.12 was required. The AS.12 lacked range, mainly due to its wire-guidance system, so the Admiralty raised a Staff Requirement,

Westland Wasp HAS1 XT780 of 705 NAS with a pair of Nord AS.12 ASMs. The Royal Navy's Westland Wasp and Wessex helicopters could be armed with the Nord AS.12 missile. AS.12 is optically tracked, with two flares to aid visibility, and commands are transferred by wire. (Terry Panopalis Collection)

NSR.6624, for its replacement. BAC won the contract and developed a missile with the designation CL.834, which was named Sea Skua when it entered service in 1982. A semi-active radar homing missile, it relies on the Lynx's Ferranti Sea Spray radar. Sea Skua has an excellent service record, seeing action in the Falklands and Operation *Telic*.

An updated Sea Skua II with active radar homing was considered, but not proceeded with. The replacement for Sea Skua was to meet the Future Anti-Surface Guided Weapon (Heavy) (FASGW(H)) and was known as Sea Venom when it entered service in 2021. Developed by MBDA, Sea Venom is carried by the Wildcat HMA2 (the Lynx replacement) and uses infrared guidance with an option for command guidance via the seeker.

The Wildcat is also armed with a smaller weapon, developed as the Lightweight Multirole Missile (LMM) to meet a requirement for a Future Anti-Surface Guided Weapon (Light) (FASGW(L)). Derived from the Thales Starstreak MVM SAM, LMM is small, light and five rounds can be carried alongside a Sea Venom on each of the Wildcat's 'Martlet wings' – detachable stub wings that support

Above: To replace the AS.12 and Wasp, the Royal Navy acquired the Westland Lynx and the Sea Skua, a semi-active homing missile that gave the helicopter a bit more scope to manoeuvre. Westland Lynx HMA8 XZ236 has released a Sea Skua, and the Redstart boost motor has yet to fire. (Blue Envoy Collection)

Left: To replace Sea Skua, MBDA has developed Sea Venom to arm the FAA's Wildcat HMA2. With a range of 11nm (20km), Sea Venom uses an infrared seeker, with an option for 'man-in-the-loop' guidance via the seeker. (Author)

two pylons apiece. Martlet is intended to attack small surface targets such as RIBs and fast attack craft with limited anti-aircraft defences.

As noted above, Martel was not exactly a success but, of course, it was designed as a general-purpose weapon rather than a dedicated anti-ship missile. HSD attempted to widen the appeal of Martel with anti-ship variants that incorporated a sea-skimming capability. HSD's air-, ship- and submarine-launched Martels were met with little enthusiasm in Whitehall, with the Admiralty opting to buy the French Aérospatiale MM.38 Exocet for its warships, and the UGM-84 Sub-Harpoon rather than the Sub-Martel for its submarines; and the Air Staff eventually chose the Harpoon for its Nimrods. During the early stages of its development, Nimrod also carried the Nord AS.12 and, for some bizarre reason, the AS.11 anti-tank missile! Handling a MCLOS wire-guided missile, like the AS.11 or AS.12 intended for helicopters, from a jet aircraft like Nimrod would have been an interesting experience in combat. Perhaps the intention was to add anti-tank to the many roles of Nimrod, but the AS.11 was more probably aimed at the colonial policing role in the original Nimrod requirement.

Above: **The Exocet was effective, and in its air-launched AM.39 guise was used against the British task force during the Falklands Conflict of 1982. This sequence shows a submarine-launched SM.39 impacting a vessel during trials. (Blue Envoy Collection)**

Right: **Not long for this aircraft. The wire-guided AS.12 was, like the TV Martel, intended to arm the Nimrod. For various reasons, including lack of range, it was never adopted. The pylons were useful and by 1982 were fitted with twin rails for Sidewinders. (A&AEE neg. A1591-1 via Phil Butler)**

Even more bizarre than the AS.12 was the testing of the AS.11 anti-tank missile on the Nimrod. The results of this trial are unknown, but suffice to say, the Nimrod had no anti-tank role. As with fitting Sidewinders, the Nimrod could have been the world's biggest tank buster. (Blue Envoy Collection)

None of these were entirely satisfactory, leaving the Nimrod MR1 with an anti-ship missile capability of sorts, but, in reality, none that were effective. By 1981, the Nimrod was being upgraded to the MR2 standard, and as these were entering service, the Falklands Conflict began. An inflight refuelling probe was added, and since the Nimrod MR2 retained the wing pylons of the earlier variant, these were modified to carry a pair of AIM-9L Sidewinders apiece. To provide a viable anti-ship capability, the weapons bay was adapted to carry the McDonnell Douglas AGM.84 Harpoon.

A maximum of two Harpoons could be carried in the Nimrod MR2's weapons bay, but when the Nimrod MRA4 was developed, its new wing acquired wing pylons for four Harpoons. When the ill-fated Nimrod MRA4 was cancelled, its replacement, the Boeing P-8A Poseidon MRA1, could also carry four Harpoons on underwing pylons.

One Martel derivative, the BAe Dynamics Sea Eagle, did enter service and became the principal weapon of the Buccaneer S2B and Tornado GR1B squadrons tasked with the maritime strike role, while the Sea Harrier FRS1 could carry a pair of Sea Eagles. The Sea Harrier FRS51s of the Indian Naval Air Arm also carried the weapon, whereas another fast jet that carried Sea Eagle was the Indian

Nimrod prototype XV148 was tested with a pair of AJ.168 TV-Martels on underwing pylons. The missile, while listed as a weapon for Nimrod, was not carried operationally. Nimrods had to wait for the MR.2 upgrade and the urgent requirement issued during the Falklands Conflict to acquire an anti-ship missile capability. The AGM-84 Harpoon was acquired, and a pair could be carried in the weapons bay. (Blue Envoy Collection)

Air Force's Jaguar IM, a dedicated maritime strike variant of the Jaguar International fitted with an Agave radar for the role.

Oddly enough, the Indian Navy also fielded Sea Eagle on its fleet of Russian Ilyushin Il-38 *May* maritime patrol aircraft, which were modified to carry Sea Eagle on pylons attached to the rear fuselage. The Indian Naval Air Arm's Sea King Mk.42s carried Sea Eagle and, like the missiles on the *May*, were fitted with a pair of boost rocket motors.

Developed by BAe Dynamics to meet AST.1226, Sea Eagle was little more than a Martel shape as it was powered by a Microturbo TRI 60 turbojet, used an active radar seeker and could fly a sea-skimming attack profile. A ship-launched version was proposed as a replacement for the MM.38 Exocet but lost out to the RGM-84 Harpoon, which has been fitted on Duke-class frigates.

Right: Sea Eagle was the ultimate development of the Martel line but shared little more than the basic airframe and configuration. Buccaneers and Tornados carried up to four Sea Eagles. Proposed derivatives were not taken up. (Blue Envoy Collection)

Below: The Hawker Siddeley Sea Harrier FRS1 could carry two Sea Eagles, and the combination entered service with the Royal and Indian navies. The Indian Navy also armed its Ilyushin Il-38 *May* maritime patrol aircraft and Sea King helicopters with Sea Eagle, in these cases, with boost rocket motors. (Blue Envoy Collection)

Above left: Comparison of this ordnance spread from the end of the Buccaneer's service with that of the start on page 20 shows how even 'legacy' aircraft could have their capability much enhanced by modern guided weapons. This Buccaneer can carry Sea Eagle ASMs, Paveway LGBs, Sidewinder AAMs, a Pave Spike designator, an AN/ALQ-101 jammer and, of course, 1,000lb free-fall bombs. The green missile is an AS.37 anti-radar Martel. (Blue Envoy Collection)

Above right: Rather than the surface-launched Ship-Martel from HSD the Admiralty opted for the Aérospatiale MM.38 Exocet to arm its ships. HMS *Fife* has just launched an Exocet from one of the four launchers that replaced the original B turret. (Blue Envoy Collection)

Below: A GWS-60 Harpoon launch from a Duke-class destroyer. Long-range anti-ship capability for HM ships is provided by the Boeing RGM-84 Harpoon, a turbojet-powered weapon that replaced the MM.38 Exocet, while the AGM-84 air-launched Harpoon arms the RAF's P-8 Poseidon MRA1. (MOD/Open Government Licence)

Chapter 7

Specialist Weapons – SEAD and Bunker Busting

'I'm gonna fly with you, and we're gonna shoot a SAM site before it shoots us? You gotta be shittin' me!'

Jack Donovan, USAF Wild Weasel Electronic Warfare Officer

While many guided weapons changed roles with relative ease, there were specific operations that required bespoke equipment. Suppression of enemy air defences (SEAD) was one such role, requiring missiles that could destroy radar equipment even if they switched off, while for the destruction of fortified installations such as hardened aircraft shelters and command bunkers, they required an approach like that of tank killing, but at a much longer range.

Defence Suppression

The Air Staff had watched with interest as air power played a pivotal role in the war in Vietnam, but as US involvement in that war wound down, another war, shorter but equally significant, influenced British thinking. While the US air arms had faced what were essentially fixed anti-aircraft weapons, the Israeli Air Force had to deal with the Soviet model of all-arms mobile warfare: armoured formations protected by mobile air defences. This was pretty much what NATO would be facing in Western Europe but on a grander scale. The USAF doctrine, which had worked in Vietnam, was to attack enemy air defence assets – suppression of enemy air defences (SEAD) using aircraft, known as Wild Weasels, dedicated to that role. While this worked well on fixed defences, the 1973 October/Yom Kippur War had shown that mobile air defences were ubiquitous and difficult to tackle, and the RAF could not afford Wild Weasels nor to have a major part of its strike force assigned to a support role.

In the 1970s, the RAF's SEAD capability was based on the AS.37 Martel, which was big (13ft 9in/4.2m long), heavy (1,210lb/550kg), slow (Mach 0.9) and not particularly reliable. To attack different radars, a new seeker had to be fitted by the groundcrew, making it inflexible as well. What was required was a flexible system that could be used by any aircraft and was compact enough to avoid taking up a stores pylon used for ground-attack weapons.

In the Vietnam War, the USAF and US Navy's weapons against radar and air defence systems were the AGM-45 Shrike and AGM-78 Standard and cluster bombs. This Republic F-105G Thunderchief Wild Weasel is fitted with both, with Shrike nearest the camera. (Author)

In April 1982, the only anti-radiation missile in the RAF inventory was the AS.37 Martel. Having been test fitted on the Victor K2, it fell to the Vulcan B2 to flight test the installation. Vulcan XM597 tested the AS.37 on the port wing pylon with a AN/ALQ-101 jamming pod on the starboard pylon. (Via Phil Butler)

US systems such as the AGM-45 Shrike and AGM-78 Standard could be spoofed by putting the radar into a dummy load (a tactic countered by switching to an inertial navigator), but their replacement, the AGM-85 High-speed Anti-Radiation Missile (HARM), relied on high speed to hit the target radar before it could take countermeasures. The RAF's Air Staff wanted a different approach and issued ASR.1228 in 1978. After a lot of discussion about how it should operate, it led to the development of the Air Launched Anti-Radiation Missile – ALARM.

BAe Dynamics' missile was small enough to be carried on the same auxiliary pylons of a Tornado or Jaguar intended for carrying Sidewinders. ALARM could be used in two modes: direct or loiter attack; in each mode, it plunged vertically onto the target before detonating its warhead, which was designed to send its blast and tungsten fragments laterally for maximum effect on radar equipment.

In loiter mode, ALARM climbed to 40,000ft (12,192m) before making a vertical dive onto its target. If the target radar detected the attack and went off air, ALARM's rocket motor would shut down and a small parachute would deploy slowing the missile's descent. If, during this loiter period, the radar resumed transmitting, the chute would be jettisoned, and the rocket relit to plunge onto the target.

Although nine ALARMs could be carried for a dedicated SEAD mission, the maximum useful load-out for a Tornado with fuel tanks in the escort role was seven. Tornado GR1 ZA354 was used for ALARM trials. (Blue Envoy Collection)

Of course, the radar could shut down again, but ALARM could re-enter loiter mode until the radar began operating and resume its attack. In direct attack mode, the missile would climb before diving onto the target.

Realistically, ALARM, like any anti-radiation missile, didn't need to destroy the radar but merely put the equipment off the air until the attack aircraft had passed out of range; however, its capabilities allowed almost any strike aircraft to perform the SEAD role.

ALARM entered RAF service in 1990 and was fielded during Operation *Granby*, but its finest hour was against Serbian air defences during Operation *Allied Force*, when a single ALARM destroyed a radar that had evaded attempts by USAF, USN and Luftwaffe forces to shut it down using HARM. Over 100 HARM launches had failed to destroy the Serbian radar. Enter a Tornado GR1 with a single ALARM. The Serb radar went off air, in the standard procedure when faced with an ARM. It was never heard from again.

Right: A BAeD ALARM just prior to detonation on a radar target. One of the keys to ALARM's success was its attack profile, which included a loiter capability followed by a vertical dive onto the target, defeating revetments and maximising blast/fragment damage. (Blue Envoy Collection)

Below: One of ALARM's advantages was that it could be carried on most strike aircraft. This Harrier GR5 is carrying two ALARMs, two Sidewinders and a pair of Paveway laser-guided bombs. (Blue Envoy Collection)

ALARM made its debut in Operation *Granby* in 1991. Tornado GR1 ZA441 in desert pink carries a pair of ALARMs on ventral pylons. (Blue Envoy Collection)

Interestingly, despite having eschewed the dedicated SEAD type, the RAF did field a 'Wild Weasel' version of the Tornado F3 as the 'EF3' that used the Tornado's Emissions Location System to provide the Tornado navigator with an overview of the radar situation, enabling targets to be selected for attack with ALARM.

ALARM was withdrawn in 2013, its role to be taken on by Selective Precision Effects At Range – Electronic Warfare (SPEAR-EW) and another of the missile systems that arose from experience in the 1990s – Storm Shadow.

The Sledgehammer

Operation *Granby* taught the RAF a lot. The JP.233 anti-runway weapon worked but exposed the delivery aircraft to anti-aircraft artillery (AAA) and, similarly, the IBL.755 took the strike aircraft into the danger zone. The problem with JP.223 was that the Iraqi airfields were huge, much bigger than the Warsaw Pact airfields it was intended to destroy, and the perimeter defences could engage the aircraft before they had egressed the target zone. Attacking armour with cluster bombs also took aircraft into the engagement envelopes of Iraqi AAA. Another lesson learned was that, aside from Paveway laser-guided bombs (LGBs), the RAF had no weapon that could attack targets such as bunkers and hardened aircraft shelters (HAS), see Appendix 2.

Before the campaign ended, RAF tactics changed from low level to medium altitude, as the SAM threat had been negated by SEAD operations. Paveway LGBs were used against hardened targets, delivered from above the effective ceiling of Iraqi AAA and MANPADS.

Two new weapons arose from Operation *Granby* and both sought the ability to strike from afar – what is known in guided weapons parlance as 'stand-off'. The navy achieved conventional stand-off with the Raytheon Tomahawk Land Attack Cruise Missile (TLAM) with a range of 1,000 miles (1,600km), while the RAF had been down this road many times before, but usually with nuclear weapons.

Above: Another weapon making its debut in Operation *Granby* was the JP233 anti-runway weapon. This required the Tornado to fly low, straight and level while delivering the submunitions. (Hunting via Terry Panopalis)

Right: During Operation *Granby*, the RAF's sole means to destroy bunkers and other hardened targets was the Paveway II. This led to the procurement of Storm Shadow and updated Paveways and designator pods. This Harrier GR9 is carrying two Paveway IVs, two Sidewinders and, on the port ventral hardpoint, a Sniper designator pod. (Blue Envoy Collection)

Below: A Tomahawk TLAM about to impact a target during trials in the USA. Targets for the TLAM can be up to 1,000 miles (1,600km) from the launch point, which provides attack capability against a vast range of land targets including hardened installations. (MOD/Open Government Licence)

Stand-off weapons had been sought since World War Two and, in RAF service, were exemplified by Blue Steel; and in the light of *Granby*, stand-off was back in favour, especially if the weapon had a 'bunker busting' capability. In 1982, the Air Staff had issued SR(A).1236, calling for a Conventional Air-launched Stand-Off Missile (CASOM) with a stand-off range of at least 216 miles (400km), autonomous guidance and a warhead that could destroy hardened structures – one of the lessons learned from *Granby*. After assessing several proposals, including a variant of the AGM-84 Harpoon called Grand Slam, a British version of MBDA's APACHE anti-runway weapon was selected and developed by MBDA as SCALP-EG and known in British service as Storm Shadow.

Storm Shadow features folding wings and is powered by a Microturbo TRI-60 turbofan for a range of 612 miles (1,000km) and has an accuracy on a par with laser-guided munitions but does not require a designator. The missile approaches the target under GPS or TERCOM (TERrain COntour Matching) guidance, and on entering the target area at low altitude, Storm Shadow performs a climb and bunt to dive onto the target. The missile's terminal guidance then takes over, jettisoning the nosecone to expose a thermographic camera that compares the image with a library of signatures. This system, Digitized Scene-Mapping Area Correlator (DSMAC), when used in conjunction with TERCOM, allows pinpoint attacks with accuracies unheard of even in the 1990s.

Storm Shadow's most interesting component is the BROACH warhead. This replaced the submunitions of APACHE with Bomb, Royal Ordnance, Augmented CHarge, which uses a tandem-charge configuration with a shaped charge to penetrate the walls and roofs of hardened structures, making a hole for a second, larger charge to enter the structure before exploding.

This new generation of air-to-ground guided weapons – Brimstone, SPEAR and Storm Shadow – coincided with the entry into service of the Typhoon and Lightning. These types, whose capabilities in the field of netcentric warfare maximise the weapons' potential, provide the RAF and FAA with the offensive clout, combined with precision, that a modern air force needs. Although Storm Shadow is not intended to be integrated with the Lightning, a more compact follow-on weapon called Future Cruise/Anti-Ship Weapon may be compatible with the type.

Above left: Intended to arm the Tornado and Typhoon the RAF's Storm Shadow differed from the SCALP-EG for the Armée de l'Air mainly in its warhead. Tornado GR4 ZA614 of 41 Sqn (the RAF's test and evaluation unit) carries four Storm Shadows on a testing sortie. (MOD/Open Government Licence)

Above right: The effect of a Storm Shadow's BROACH warhead on a reinforced concrete target. The first charge punches through the wall, allowing the second charge to pass through the hole and detonate inside. (Blue Envoy Collection)

Chapter 8
Tank Killing

'A kick in the teeth for British industry.'

A BAC executive on the MOD buying Milan

Generally, guided weapons development is a case of producing a specialised weapon for a specific role, with the other subsequent roles 'discovered' as the weapon enters service. Brimstone is a fine example of this, having started out to fill one of the most difficult roles in warfare – anti-tank.

Tanks are armoured, move rather quickly, and are generally difficult to acquire when camouflaged and obscured by clouds of smoke or the general fog of war. They also shoot back, making them hard targets in every sense of the word.

Traditionally, if a history of just over a century can be called a tradition, tanks were destroyed by hitting them with a high-velocity hardened projectile shot from a gun. These are kinetic warheads. As tanks acquired thicker armour in World War Two and then technically resistant composite armour such as the British Chobham or Russian Combination K in the Cold War, new ways to defeat them were required. These included shaped charges and self-forging/explosively formed penetrators, the chemical warheads.

The chemical warheads lend themselves to guided weapons, as these normally lack the velocity of a gun-fired projectile. Shaped charges, also known as hollow charge or HEAT (high-explosive anti-tank), were used on infantry weapons such as the PIAT, Panzerfaust and bazooka. Compact, lightweight and effective, they were selected for early guided weapons. These warheads work by surrounding a cone of metal, such as copper, with explosive. When the explosive detonates, the metal cone forms a focused plasma jet that burns through armour.

The goal of anti-tank warfare – killing tanks. A burned-out Iraqi T-72 lies in a roadside ditch along a road leading to Al-Iskandariyah, Iraq, during Operation *Telic*. (DoD)

However, the British General Staff preferred another type of warhead called HESH (high-explosive squash head) that essentially pancaked onto the vehicle before exploding. This was to be used in British anti-tank missiles, but to counter heavily armoured tanks such as the Soviet T-10, the warhead had to be large, leading to big missiles, such as Fairey's Orange William and Australian Malkara that required specialist vehicles to carry and launch them.

What was required was a guided weapon for use by the infantry for which Pye proposed Python. Unfortunately, despite possessing some innovative features such as thrust vector control (TVC), at 5ft (1.4m) long, weighing 81lb (36.8kg) and with a large launch frame, it took two strapping lads to move it about.

Vickers had other ideas, producing something more akin to a guided Panzerfaust: portable, launched from a small carry case and simple to operate. Vigilant (VIsually Guided Infantry Light ANti-Tank) used a similar manual guidance system to Malkara (visually tracked and wire guided), but its controls gave a smoother response than Malkara making it easier to use at short range. Weighing in at 31lb (14kg),

Left:The army was keen to get guided weapons, and one role that was ideal, given the threat from Warsaw Pact tank armies, was the anti-tank guided weapon. Malkara was a curious mix of Australian and British technology. This example has just been launched from a FV4010 mock-up. Malkara was not exactly compact. (Blue Envoy Collection)

Below: Pye developed the Python, an infantry anti-tank guided weapon. It was a bit bulky to be moved around, but it was a start. This infantryman is in position to support an attack by armour, including the Centurion tank in the background. (Blue Envoy Collection)

Vickers intended Vigilant to be carried by infantrymen, set up and ready for action in minutes. Up to six Vigilants could be connected to a single launch control box, allowing a single soldier to switch between missiles deployed along a front, potentially knocking out six tanks.

The revolutionary thinking that one squaddie could knock out almost half a squadron of tanks was not well received in all quarters. When two Vickers engineers presented Vigilant to General 'Pete' Pyman, the formidable Deputy Chief of the Imperial General Staff reportedly chased them out of his office! Pyman died in 1971, so did not witness the success of the Soviet AT-3 *Sagger*, the Soviet analogue of Vigilant, against Israeli armour in October 1973.

To replace Vigilant, in a gesture towards European solidarity, and much to the chagrin of BAC, the MOD bought the Franco-German Milan. BAC cried foul and pointed out that Savig, its updated Vigilant that used the SACLOS guidance from Rapier, was cheaper, more effective and used existing infrastructure. The MOD would not be swayed; it bought Milan and its finest hour was demolishing sangars in the Falklands. One BAC executive described the procurement of Milan as 'a kick in the teeth for British industry'.

Right: In contrast with Malkara, Vickers' Vigilant was small, fairly light and hard hitting. It was more easily concealed than the Hornet-mounted Malkara, and rather than two rounds on a specialised vehicle, any vehicle could carry many Vigilants. (Blue Envoy Collection)

Below left: The idea that one squaddie could destroy six tanks was anathema to the upper echelons of the tank-oriented General Staff. The simplicity of Vigilant is apparent here as an infantryman awaits his targets. (Blue Envoy Collection)

Below right: As a successor for Vigilant, the Milan proved bulkier as it required a separate firing post. It was highly successful as a sangar-buster during the Falklands Conflict in 1982. (Blue Envoy Collection)

All the effort on Python and Orange William was not wasted and in the mergers of the aircraft companies in the late 1950s, Fairey's guided weapons division became part of BAC (Guided Weapons). Prior to the merger, Fairey had embarked on Project 12, a heavier, wire-guided, anti-tank missile for the Royal Armoured Corps (RAC). The aim was a missile that would be easier to 'gather' after launch by having a slow launch speed and control via TVC like Python and hit hard with a large HEAT warhead. Post-merger, this became the BAC Swingfire, and at twice the weight of Vigilant was best used from vehicles. However, thanks to its slow launch and TVC, these launch vehicles could be concealed while the operator operated the missile from a position away from the launcher.

Having entered service with the RAC in 1969, Swingfire and its FV.438 and FV.102 Striker vehicles, and their roles, were transferred to the Royal Horse Artillery. The FV.438 was a modified FV.432 armoured personnel carrier with two launch 'bins' that were reloadable from inside the vehicle, with a further 12 rounds in racks ready to load. Striker carried five Swingfires ready to launch but had to be reloaded from outside. Striker was air-portable in a C-130 Hercules or underslung from a Chinook, making it a mobile and heavy hitting asset on the battlefield. Striker and its Swingfires served until 2005, with its last campaign being Operation *Telic* in 2003.

Swingfire could be mounted on a variety of vehicles, including Land Rovers (called Beeswing, as it was mounted on a B-class vehicle) and hovercraft, with one version of Swingfire aimed at arming helicopters. Hawkswing was to equip the Westland Lynx for the anti-tank role, but since the Swingfire left its bins at 45 degrees then levelled out, trials discovered that at altitudes under 250ft (76m), the missile tended to hit the ground after launch. It was also too slow, its flight time making the Lynx vulnerable to Warsaw Pact mobile AAA and SAMs while the Hawkswing flew towards its target.

Another problem encountered later on in Swingfire's service was the addition of explosive reactive armour (ERA) on Soviet tanks. This comprises blocks of explosive attached to the tank hull and turret which, when hit by the plasma jet from a HEAT warhead, explode to negate the effect of the incoming warhead. The counter to ERA is a tandem charge that uses a primary charge to trigger the ERA followed by the secondary charge that penetrates the vehicle armour.

Another missile that entered service in the 1960s was Swingfire, the successor to the unwieldy Malkara. In the 1970s, Swingfire was mounted on the FV.102 Striker, which carried five rounds in a launcher on the back of the vehicle. (Blue Envoy Collection)

Right: A Hawkswing leaves its launch bin during trials on a Scout AH1. To replace the SS.11 and arm the Westland Lynx in the anti-tank role, BAC proposed Hawkswing – an air-launched Swingfire. It was heavy, slow and tended to hit the ground if launched too low. (Blue Envoy Collection)

Below: The Soviet T-72 (known to NATO intelligence as the NST) was well armoured with composite armour and explosive reactive armour modules on the glacis plate and turret. This Indian Army Ajeya Mk.2 is typical of the armour fit of the T-72. (Vivek Patankar/CC BY 2.0 via Wikimedia Commons)

While the Hawkswing was being proposed, tested and dismissed, the British Army fielded the Nord SS.11 anti-tank missile on its Scout AH1 helicopters. These served with distinction and were used with great success in the Falklands Conflict. Having been stripped of the missile kit to use them as utility machines, the Scouts had it replaced in the field while the rotors turned, which took hot refuelling and rearming to the extreme. The SS.11s were then used to silence Argentine field guns that had been bombarding British troops.

As mentioned above, the air-launched variant of Swingfire failed to prosper. In its lieu, the Army Air Corps was equipped with the Hughes TOW (Tube-launched, Optically tracked, Wire-guided) anti-tank missile. The TOW was faster, lighter, and rather than six Hawkswings, eight TOWs could be mounted on the Lynx AH1(TOW). Like Swingfire, TOW was not suitable for use against ERA and was updated to handle reactive and composite armour as the Improved TOW (ITOW). It was further improved by Britain's Thorn EMI and the Royal Ordnance Factories as the imaginatively named Further Improved TOW (FITOW) with two self-forging warheads and a laser fuse that allowed 'top attack' whereby the missile flies over the target to attack the thinner top armour of vehicles.

By the early 1980s, the General Staff were looking for a replacement for the Milan, Swingfire and TOW. It also wanted a dedicated anti-tank helicopter and sought a new missile for this new attack helicopter. The French and German armies had a similar requirement, so the three countries embarked on a new anti-tank missile, developed by Euromissile. Well… two, both called Trigat, which was a contraction of 'third-generation anti-tank'. Trigat-MR was a medium-range weapon for the infantry and vehicles, while Trigat-LR was a longer-range weapon for helicopters. Both missiles used a passive imaging infrared seeker with TV back-up and had a secondary anti-helicopter capability.

Above left: **The traditional inter-service rivalry was exemplified by the RAF objecting to the Army Air Corps' helicopters carrying weapons. By the late 1960s, they had all but given up, and the AAC armed its Scouts with the SS.11 in the anti-tank role. This Westland Scout AH1 has just launched an SS.11. (Blue Envoy Collection)**

Above right: **The 1980s saw the Scout/SS.11 replaced by the Lynx AH1(TOW) with eight TOWs on weapons carriers with a further eight reloads in the cabin. This pair of Lynx helicopters shows the TOW installation and the all-important M69 sight above the cabin. (Blue Envoy Collection)**

Above: Trigat was to be a multi-function missile capable of tackling tanks and aircraft. Unfortunately, it never lived up to expectations and only the German Army use it (as the PARS-3) on their Tiger helicopters. This Euromissile artwork shows Trigat in action against armoured vehicles and helicopters. (Blue Envoy Collection)

Right: In the 1990s, there were high hopes for a missile called Trigat (Third-Generation Anti-Tank) to arm infantry, vehicles and helicopters. This Trigat-LR, aimed for helicopter use, has just left its launch tube. (Blue Envoy Collection)

In 1995, the British Army opted for the Westland WAH-64D Apache attack helicopter, and it came with Hellfire, specifically the AGM-114L Longbow variant that uses a millimetre wave radar seeker. The UK withdrew from Trigat-LR in 1995, as it had not been integrated with the Apache, and France withdrew in 2004, citing delays with Trigat-LR, leaving Germany to keep the faith. The laser-guided Trigat-MR fared little better, but the UK's patience finally ran out in 2000, and the US FGM-148 Javelin was procured to replace both Swingfire and Milan from 2003.

Not to be confused with the Shorts Javelin MANPADS, the replacement for Swingfire is the anti-tank Javelin, a fire-and-forget top-attack missile with a 5in (127mm) diameter HEAT warhead and infrared guidance. Described as portable, Javelin is quite weighty for a single infantryman, so it is usually served by two crew and can be mounted on a tripod. To replace Milan, the British Army selected NLAW (New generation Lightweight Anti-tank Weapon) a collaborative project involving SAAB-Bofors Dynamics of Sweden and Thales Air Defence (formerly Shorts). NLAW is half the weight of a Javelin, and due to

Left: A pair of WAH-64 Apache AH1s seen here carrying 19-round pods for CRV7 rockets and Hellfire drill rounds, the latter identifiable by their blue colour. The radome on the rotor mast contains the antenna for the Longbow radar. (MOD/Open Government Licence)

Below: Having cancelled the medium range Trigat, the MOD opted to acquire the US Javelin ATGW. This Javelin has just left its launcher, the flip-out fins have deployed, and the rocket motor has just ignited. (MOD/Open Government Licence)

The SAAB/Bofors/Thales NLAW has replaced Milan in the British Army as the lightweight anti-armour weapon. With little or no backblast, NLAW can be fired from enclosed spaces such as buildings. (MOD/Open Government Licence)

its 'soft launch' can be fired from confined spaces. The missile uses a guidance called predicted line of sight (PLOS), whereby the operator tracks the target for three seconds and the system calculates where the target will be when the missile impacts.

Tank Busting from the Air

General Pyman's disbelief that a mere squaddie was capable of destroying his main battle tanks is understandable, and he may have had a point. In the 1950s, destroying tanks with expensive aircraft and their pilots was not very successful, so how could an infantryman do what cutting-edge aircraft could not? That was certainly the case until the 1990s. The difference was precision guidance and 'smart' munitions and far from being just 'tank plinkers', the 21st century's air-launched anti-tank missiles are set to revolutionise air warfare.

The RAF's change of focus to Europe also drove change in the air support force's weaponry, while the change from massive nuclear retaliation to 'Flexible Response' in 1961 drove a move towards conventional weapons for use against tanks. Rather than using tactical nuclear weapons against Warsaw Pact armoured formations (whose response had been to spread out), attacks on small units or even individual vehicles was now the norm. The BL.755 anti-tank cluster bomb and the SNEB rocket were the RAF's main weapons against armour, but Warsaw Pact armour had defences against the RAF.

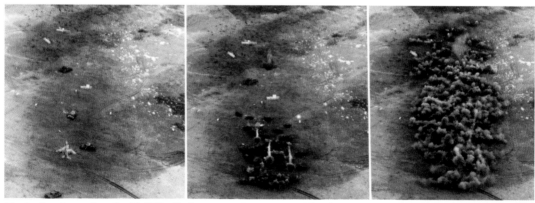

Cluster bombs such as the BL.755 relied on saturating an area with submunitions. By the 1980s, the anti-armour submunitions were not capable of destroying the new generation of Soviet tanks. A Jaguar delivers a BL.755 on a formation of tanks on a firing range. (Blue Envoy Collection)

The burgeoning Warsaw Pact armoured forces were accompanied by mobile air defences such as the SA-6 *Gainful* SAM system and ZSU-23/4 Shilka SPAAG, both of which posed a threat to NATO air forces. This was ably demonstrated in the 1973 October/Yom Kippur War when Egyptian and Syrian *Gainful* and Shilkas took a heavy toll on Israeli aircraft.

The answer was to be a precision anti-armour guided weapon and a missile to shut down the air defence systems – what became known as an anti-radiation missile (ARM). Requirements were issued – ASR.1238 for the former and ASR.1228 for the latter – but these would take time to develop, especially the anti-armour weapon. This was mainly due to improvements in Soviet tanks, with new types such as the New Soviet Tank (NST, became the T-64 and T-72) and the Future Soviet Tank (FST, became the T-80). These were resistant to the BL.755 submunitions and SNEB, so a new submunition was developed, for what became known as Improved BL.755, an interim weapon pending the deployment of the ASR.1238 weapon.

The outcome of ASR.1238 is Brimstone, a fire-and-forget missile developed by GEC-Marconi, which merged into MBDA, and has produced a family of weapons in use around the world and on a variety of platforms. The key to Brimstone was its seeker, a millimetre wave (MMW) active radar type that could home in on vehicles, particularly tanks spread across a battlefield, and destroy them. Described as semi-autonomous, Brimstone could be launched into a target area and then select its target based on the signatures and decided how best to attack it. As the battlefield changed from hitting T-80s on the North German Plain to striking 'technicals' on the busy streets of Libyan towns, Brimstone also changed, adopting a new dual-mode seeker that could be switched from active MMW radar to laser seeking, allowing individual vehicles in a busy roadway to be designated and targeted.

Brimstone was a complex system, and despite the original requirement being issued in 1982, the weapon did not enter service until 2005 and made its operational debut during Operation *Ellamy*, destroying technicals and armour operated by Libyan rebels. During this protracted development of Brimstone, and with experience from the Kosovo War, the Air Staff sought a stopgap weapon to arm the Harrier GR5, 7 and 9. The AGM-65 Maverick was acquired and was used by Harriers in Operation *Telic* in 2003.

SR(A).1238 was intended to provide strike aircraft such as Harriers with a precision anti-armour capability. This Harrier GR5 carries 12 Brimstone prototypes, two Sidewinders for self-protection and a pair of external fuel tanks. (Blue Envoy Collection)

Right: The active radar seeker of Brimstone operates on a narrow beam width, which reduces its susceptibility to detection and jamming. This Dual Mode Brimstone can also use laser designation for more precise targeting. (MOD/Open Government Licence)

Below: Acquired in the light of delays with Brimstone, the AGM-65G2 model was optimised for anti-armour and armed the Harriers pending delivery of Brimstone. Harrier GR9 ZD470 of No 1 (Fighter) Sqn cuts a dash, showing off its AGM-65G2 Maverick in the skies above RAF Akrotiri, Cyprus. (MOD/Open Government Licence)

One characteristic of guided weapons that always requires improvement is range, and MBDA addressed this in Brimstone with SPEAR (Selective Precision Effects At Range). Developed as Brimstone 2 for the RAF to increase the missile's range, SPEAR provides additional stand-off capability for the Typhoon, Lightning and any hardware that emerges from the Tempest programme. SPEAR involves replacing the rocket motor with a Hamilton Sundstrand TJ-150 turbojet and adding a wing kit to the basic airframe which, when combined with INS/GPS guidance, produced a precision weapon with a range of 80 miles (130km). SPEAR can be carried on a variety of strike aircraft and thanks to its folding wings can be carried on the same triple racks as Brimstone and internally by the RAF/FAA Lockheed F-35B Lightnings.

Brimstone and SPEAR could be described as the multi-role combat weapon of the early 21st century, as it encompasses roles ranging from anti-tank, precision strike, long-range attack, anti-ship and even SEAD.

From its beginnings as an anti-tank missile for use against Warsaw Pact armour, Brimstone has gone from strength to strength. Dual Mode Brimstone brings laser precision to an already precise weapon and the addition of a turbofan and wing kit provides SPEAR with the same capability with long range. (Author)

The United States has long been wedded to the nuclear triad whereby the deterrent is to be delivered by silo-based ICBMs (a mode already dismissed by the British government), submarine-launched ballistic missiles (SLBMs) and weapons delivered by aircraft. The British had no such luxury as the nuclear triad and had to choose one delivery system for its nuclear deterrent, ie strategic weapons. Tactical nuclear weapons, on the other hand, could be delivered by a variety of means, including Blue Peacock – a truck-mounted nuclear land mine kept warm by chickens.

Although the RAF did not field Blue Streak, one strategic weapon that was deployed by the RAF was the Douglas Thor Intermediate-Range Ballistic Missile (IRBM). This was operated by Bomber Command on a dual-key basis, meaning the UK could operate and maintain but not launch Thors without American permission. With a range of 1,500 miles (2,400km), the RAF's Thor bases in England's East Midlands put Warsaw Pact targets in eastern Europe and the western Soviet Union in range of ballistic attack with Thor. The missiles were delivered in 1958 and, as was the state of the art, had to be fuelled before launch, thus making them vulnerable to a first strike. By 1963, US intercontinental ballistic missiles could target the areas covered by Thor, and so the RAF returned its Thors to the US.

Thor was operated under a dual-key system by the RAF, on RAF bases and maintained by RAF personnel. They were deployed in 1958 but by 1963 had all been returned to the US. (Blue Envoy Collection)

One USAF project to develop an arm of the triad, one that the RAF was keen to become involved with, was the air-launched ballistic missile (ALBM) and even before Blue Streak was cancelled, the RAF had a presence in the development teams of what became the Douglas Skybolt. Launched from a bomber flying at 45,000ft (13,716m) the two-stage Skybolt was boosted into a ballistic trajectory before shedding its first stage to continue upwards to a point downrange where the missile was slowed. Forward-facing vents on the second-stage motor were used to arrest the vehicle and thus control the range of the re-entry vehicle (RV). Skybolt could hit a target 1,000 miles (1,609km) from the launch point and a Boeing B-52 Stratofortress could carry up to four missiles.

The Air Staff was smitten. Skybolt, carried by Vulcans and Victors, was the answer to its prayers, as it would extend the lives of the V-bombers, keeping them viable for at least another decade and deliver RAF officers from a life underground. Interestingly, that supposed advocate of all things in the world of guided weapons, Duncan Sandys, wasn't keen on Skybolt, as he considered the V-bombers just as vulnerable to a first strike as Blue Streak. The Air Staff responded that they would eventually be operated on a continuous airborne alert basis as patrol missile carriers, for which a civil servant coined the term 'Poffler'. Skybolt was ordered for the RAF and plans were afoot for a new fleet of aircraft such as modified Avro Vulcans and Vickers VC10s to carry up to eight Skybolts and operate as Pofflers.

The third arm of the US nuclear triad was especially attractive to the Admiralty who, having seen the RAF take on the deterrent role with the V-force, was keen on the 'Senior Service' regaining its status in the British war machine. A contemporary of Skybolt, Lockheed's Polaris submarine-launched ballistic missile was undergoing trials at the same time as Skybolt and was suffering some development problems. However, unlike Skybolt, these had been expected, came as no surprise and had been planned for. Such is life in weapons development.

Having cancelled all other options, 144 Skybolts were ordered, with 72 examples required initially, two for each Vulcan B2S (the Skybolt-carrying variant). The Admiralty shared Sandys' concerns, but that argument was countered with the observation that, with 16 missiles on board, putting the deterrent in four submarines rather than 36 aircraft was akin to putting all your eggs in one basket.

Avro began work on integrating Skybolt with the Vulcan B2S in May 1960 and by December 1961, dummy Skybolts were being dropped by Vulcan XH538 over the Solway Firth in southwest

Framed by its stablemate in the test programme, Vulcan B2 XH537 carries two dummy Skybolts. The replacement for the silo-based Blue Streak ballistic missile (and Blue Steel) was intended to be the Douglas Skybolt air-launched ballistic missile. Its cancellation triggered what passed for panic in the British Civil Service. (Blue Envoy Collection)

Scotland and all was looking rosy. By late 1962, another leg of the US triad was gaining momentum, as the Minuteman ICBM was showing promise and allowed the USAF to deliver warheads to targets in the Soviet Union from silos in the American Midwest. President John F Kennedy's Secretary of Defense, Robert McNamara, arrived in office in January 1961, determined to streamline US weapons procurement and had the USAF's plethora of weapons systems in his sights. Skybolt was one of those and, in the light of its development problems, was cancelled in December 1962. By this time, Polaris had been in service in US Navy George Washington-class boats for more than a year and, aside from the usual shakedown problems, was operating well.

A Lockheed UGM-27 Polaris A3 powers skyward after launch from a submerged submarine. By 1962, there really was only one option for the UK deterrent – submarine-launched ballistic missiles. On the cancellation of Skybolt, the US president, John F Kennedy offered Prime Minister Harold Macmillan the Polaris system. Macmillan welcomed it with open arms. (MOD/Open Government Licence)

This left the British government with a bit of a problem, as the country would now be without the credible deterrent that the government had repeatedly stated it required. In a hastily arranged summit at Nassau in the Bahamas, President Kennedy and Prime Minister Harold Macmillan signed the Nassau Agreement, which allowed Britain to acquire the Polaris A3 missile, re-entry vehicles, missile tubes and fire control systems and install them in British *Resolution*-class submarines. The re-entry vehicles would be fitted with British warheads, derived from the American devices, but that would not be the end of British modification of the Polaris system.

A Horse Under Water

'You couldn't spread them about a bit?'

Admiralty request to the Chevaline development team.

The UK's deterrent policy hinged on what was called the Moscow Criterion which, in short, alluded to the ability to place a nuclear weapon on or above the Soviet capital. When the USSR fielded its ABM-1 *Galosh* anti-ballistic missile system, the capability of Polaris A3 was questioned. The US solution was to develop the Poseidon system with multiple independently-targeted re-entry vehicles (MIRVs), but the British lacked the funds to completely replace Polaris with Poseidon.

The solution was to develop a new warhead carrier or 'bus' for Polaris that could defeat the *Galosh* and its *Dog House* and *Cat House* acquisition radar systems. Like Churchill before her, Prime Minister Margaret Thatcher was quite taken aback by the steps the earlier Labour governments, under Wilson and Callaghan, had taken to make improvements to the deterrent. Under a project called Chevaline, the RAE and various industries, had, in complete secrecy, developed a new final stage for the Polaris. Prime Minister Thatcher was aghast at the cost when its existence was revealed, but its development was too far advanced to cancel.

Chevaline was fielded by the Royal Navy in 1982 and comprised a penetration aids carrier and two warheads. It included a countermeasures dispenser that carried chaff to blind the defending radars and decoys that mimicked the radar return of the RVs. Many of these countermeasures were originally developed for Blue Streak and tested using the Black Knight test vehicle in the late 1950s and early 1960s. To date, no other ballistic missile system has used such countermeasures, although the Russian 9K720 Iskander (SS-21 *Scarab*) is thought to have used decoys during attacks on Ukraine in March 2022.

Development of the systems for Chevaline, including the bus, used a test vehicle called Fallstaff, and these and other tests revealed that the

The Chevaline programme was one of the most secret projects undertaken by the British government. Now a museum piece, the Chevaline Penetration Aids Carrier (PAC) was a very sophisticated spacecraft. The black cone-shaped object is one of the two re-entry vehicles. (Author)

system was very accurate, possibly too accurate as it was said to be able to deliver two warheads into the same street. This revelation prompted the request quoted at the head of this chapter, for which the solution was to cant the two warheads outwards once the nose shroud had been shed.

Chevaline suffered many delays but, like Blue Steel before it, can be viewed as a triumph of British innovation and engineering. It was deployed on the Polaris boats as the continuous at-sea nuclear deterrent until it was replaced by the Trident D5 system from 1993. Trident possesses intercontinental range, which allows it to be launched from a wider area of ocean than earlier missiles, thus posing a greater problem for the ships, submarines and aircraft tasked with finding, and potentially destroying, the SSBN fleets. Each Trident missile can carry up to 16 RVs, but the exact number deployed is never revealed.

Trident has and will remain the delivery system for Britain's nuclear deterrent for the foreseeable future. The first Vanguard-class boat deployed on patrol in 1993 and, as of 2022, the replacement for Trident D5 is the Trident D5LE (Life Extension) as used by the US Navy. The system will be included in the new Dreadnought-class boats being built for the Royal Navy and is expected to enter service in the early 2030s.

Her Majesty's submarines deploy another airflight guided weapon in the shape of the Raytheon TLAM (Tomahawk Land Attack Missile), a 1,000-mile (1,609km) range cruise missile with a conventional warhead. Tomahawks have been in Royal Navy service since 1996, with continual updates including the latest Block IV. TLAM has been used in the 1999 Kosovo War, operations *Telic*, *Herrick* and *Ellamy* and made precision attack on targets far inland, thus avoiding the need for long-range attacks by aircraft.

Having breached the surface, the rocket motor fires on a Trident II D5 submarine-launched ballistic missile during post-overhaul trials of HMS *Vanguard*. Tridents feature a circular plate on the end of the nose spike to reduce drag. (MOD/Open Government Licence)

HMS *Vigilant* underway in the Firth of Clyde. One of four Vanguard-class boats that carry the UK's continuous at-sea deterrent, *Vigilant* can carry up to 16 Trident II D5 ballistic missiles, although generally only eight are carried. The boats operate from Her Majesty's Naval Base, Clyde, (HMS *Neptune*) on the Gare Loch. (MOD/Open Government Licence)

A Boeing UGM-109 Tomahawk TLAM climbs into the air under rocket boost after launch from HMS *Astute*. Once the TLAM has been boosted clear of the surface, a Williams turbofan takes over for the cruise phase of the flight. Royal Navy submarines are armed with the Block IV variant. (MOD/Open Government Licence)

Chapter 10

Backfire to Lance – The Army's Ballistic Missiles

'Never let me down.'

Martin Gore, 1987

In late December 1944, one sound remained unheard in the sky above the forests of the Ardennes – aeroengines. In the post-war analysis of the Ardennes Campaign, Allied generals, particularly British staff officers, concluded that they would no longer rely on weather-dependent air power. They had seen how the German V-2 had been used as a tactical weapon against the port facilities of Antwerp and the Ludendorff Bridge at Remagen. They wanted a similar capability and, if used as long-range artillery, there would be no need for air support, and they would never be let down again.

Britain's military scientists strove to acquire and test German equipment, gathering up aircraft to fly back to Farnborough for test flights and analyses, but they were also interested in the V-2. By October 1945, the engineering team had gathered equipment and personnel to conduct three test launches of V-2s under the codename Operation *Backfire*.

The first post-war tactical/bombardment missile on the Guided Weapons Committee's list of rocket weapons was Hammer, essentially a V-2, with another called Half Pint that was to be used like long-range artillery. By the mid-1950s, and with the engineering challenges starting to be addressed, a surface-to-surface rocket called Black Rock was to be developed by the English Electric Co (EECo) at Luton. While this is mentioned in archive material, details of Black Rock have yet to emerge, but it must have been a challenge, as the War Office turned to America for its ballistic missile needs by acquiring the Firestone Tire and Rubber Company's MGM-5 Corporal in 1953, to be maintained by English Electric. Corporal was a rather complex weapon to use in the field. Like the V-2, it required a launch platform, which had to be towed into position and levelled; then the missile was lifted and placed on the platform with the aid of a crane. The warhead and guidance systems had to be configured and, being in the nose, required a cherry picker to access it. Essentially, Corporal took time to set up and was accompanied by a caravan of support vehicles.

Interestingly, Corporal's range of 30–80 miles (48–129km) had an unexpected consequence on the UK. The test range for missiles is on Benbecula in the Outer Hebrides, with a tracking station on Hirta, St Kilda. The Soviets would sail their surveillance ships close to the range and, with fears they might set up their kit on Rockall, a granite islet 187 miles (300km) west of St Kilda, the Macmillan government claimed Rockall as part of the United Kingdom.

With Black Rock scrapped in favour of Corporal, the next tactical missile from Luton was a replacement for Corporal, a 30-mile (48km) range rocket called Red Rose. This was effectively a bombardment variant of the Red Shoes SAM, sharing its configuration and launch equipment but dismissed by the General Staff who sent the engineers back to the drawing board. They returned with Red Rose *Ab Intitio*, a vertical launch, two-stage missile transported by and launched from a 10-ton 6x6 truck. Meanwhile, Vickers was working on a similar rocket, which it called the '35-mile Weapon', which could be carried on an articulated truck or by a lightly armoured 8x8 off-road vehicle. Unlike Corporal or Red Rose, the 35-mile Weapon was launched from the back of the truck, at a comparatively shallow angle for a ballistic missile.

Left: The Royal Artillery's first operational ballistic missile was Corporal. Operated along the same lines as the German V-2, it required fuelling before launch, making its tactical flexibility limited. A Corporal lifts off from its launch stand during an exercise. (US Army/DoD)

Below: A Blue Water fire unit comprised a Bedford truck transporter erector launcher and a Land Rover with the computer systems. The soldier on the left will use the theodolite to align the guidance system's stabilised platform with the target. This is connected to the launcher by an umbilical, as is the Land Rover. (Blue Envoy Collection)

Appendix 1

Guided Weapons Companies in the United Kingdom

Most of the major aircraft companies operating in the UK at the end of World War Two became involved in guided weapons at some time. Fifteen years later, in the period of mergers during which the British government encouraged (or forced, depending on who you talk to) the companies to join forces and consolidate effort, there emerged three companies: Hawker Siddeley Dynamics (HSD); British Aircraft Corporation, Guided Weapons Division, (BAC(GW)); and Short Brothers (universally known as Shorts).

In 1977, the British government nationalised the aviation industry as British Aerospace (BAe), with the merged HSD and BAC(GW) joining forces to become British Aerospace Dynamics (BAeD). In 1996, BAeD and the French company Matra Défence merged to become Matra BAe Dynamics (MBD). The major French company EADS Aérospatiale Matra joined the consortium in 1998. The 'A' in MBDA arrived in 2001 when Alenia Marconi Systems (which included GEC-Marconi and Alenia-Difesa) joined and the company became known as MBDA. MBDA's headquarters is in Le Plessis-Robinson, southwest of Paris.

Meanwhile, in 1993, Shorts became a joint venture between Bombardier and Thompson CSF. The missile division of Shorts became Shorts Missile Systems, but in 2000, Bombardier sold its share to Thompson CSF, which was renamed Thales in 2001. The guided weapons division of Thales became Thales Air Defence in 2001.

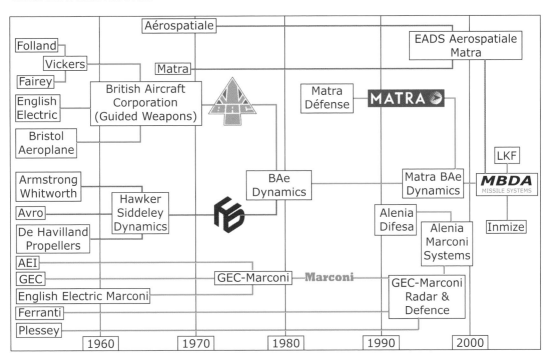

Appendix 2

Paveway Laser-guided Bombs

The Paveway I laser-guided bomb (LGB), first used by the USAF in Vietnam during 1972, was a mature technology by the early 1980s. In 1980, the RAF was fitting Paveway II guidance kits on 1,000lb bombs but target designation relied on either Pave Spike-equipped Buccaneers (of which there was a grand total of six) or troops on the ground with portable laser designators, the technique used in the Falklands Conflict. Paveway II guidance kits used 'bang-bang' controls to guide the bomb onto the target by deflecting the control surfaces to their full extent, resulting in an overcorrection that is countered by reversing the surfaces. This induced snaking in the bomb as it descended, meaning it was unsuitable for small targets such as tanks. Paveway III used proportional controls that enabled a smoother trajectory and thus did not snake, but it still relied on a second aircraft to designate targets, typified by the Buccaneer/Tornado/Paveway operations in Operation *Granby* during 1991. Since 2008, RAF aircraft and Predator UAVs have carried the Paveway IV LGB, which incorporates GPS and inertial guidance.

To replace the Pave Spike, RAF strike aircraft were equipped with new designation pods, such as the TIALD (Thermal Imaging Airborne Laser Designator) designator pod. Although rushed into service for *Granby*, it was widely used in *Telic*. Later, during the war in Afghanistan, Tornados and Harriers carried the American Sniper or LITENING III designator pods, which were considered superior to TIALD for operations in built-up areas.

SEPECAT Jaguar GR1mod XX108 undergoing Paveway trials carries a TIALD designator pod for the 1,000lb Paveway LGB on the port inboard pylon. The port outboard pylon is carrying an AN/ALQ-101 jamming pod, while the starboard outboard pylon carries a Phimat chaff dispenser. (Blue Envoy Collection)

Glossary

AAA	Anti-aircraft artillery
AAM	Air-to-air missile
Active homing	Missile carries its own radar to illuminate the target
APC	Armoured personnel carrier
Armed helicopter	Gunship, a transport helicopter fitted with weapons, eg Lynx AH1(TOW)
ASM	Anti-ship missile
Attack helicopter	Dedicated anti-tank/battlefield support helicopter, eg Apache AH1
BAC(GW)	British Aircraft Corporation (Guided Weapons)
BAeD	British Aerospace Dynamics
Beam guidance	missile flies along a light or radar beam that tracks the target
BVR	Beyond visual range
Command guidance	target and missile observed visually or by radar and missile directed to bring them together
EECo	English Electric Company
ERA	Explosive reactive armour
Fire and forget	once locked onto a target, the missile homes in with no further operator intervention
GPS	Global positioning system
HSD	Hawker Siddeley Dynamics
IFF	Identification friend or foe
MANPADS	Man-portable air defence system
MCLOS	Manual command to line of sight
PIAT	Projector, Infantry, Anti-Tank
PLOS	Predicted line of sight
QRA	Quick Reaction Alert
RAE	Royal Aircraft Establishment
RIB/RHIB	Rigid inflatable boat/rigid hull inflatable boat
RV	Re-entry vehicle
SACLOS	Semi-automatic command to line of sight
SAM	Surface-to-air missile
SARH	Semi-active radar homing (missile homes in on reflected radar energy from launcher's radar)
SEAD	Suppression of enemy air defences
STAAG	Stabilised Tachometric Anti-Aircraft Gun
Technical	Improvised fighting vehicle (essentially a pickup truck with a heavy machine gun mounted on the back)
TVC	Thrust vector control (control surfaces deflect the rocket efflux)
WRETAR	Weapons Research Establishment Target Recorder (camera system for recording missile trials)

Other books you might like:

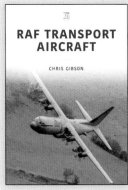

Modern Military Aircraft
Series, Vol. 6

Modern Military Aircraft
Series, Vol. 4

Modern Military Aircraft
Series, Vol. 3

Historic Military Aircraft
Series, Vol. 10

Historic Military Aircraft
Series, Vol. 8

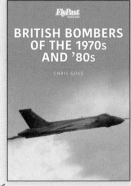

Historic Military Aircraft
Series, Vol. 4

For our full range of titles please visit:
shop.keypublishing.com/books